Faith Under Fire

*Challenges to faith embedded
in the story of a small town family.*

by Henry Wiebe

*"Always be prepared to give an answer to
everyone who asks you to give the reason for
the hope that you have." 1 Peter 3:15*

xulon PRESS

Copyright © 2010 by Henry G. Wiebe

Faith Under Fire
by Henry G. Wiebe

Printed in the United States of America

ISBN 9781609572068

All rights reserved solely by the author. The author guarantees all contents are original and do not infringe upon the legal rights of any other person or work. No part of this book may be reproduced in any form without the permission of the author. The views expressed in this book are not necessarily those of the publisher.

Unless otherwise indicated, Bible quotations are taken from The New International Version of the Bible. Copyright © 1978 by New York International Bible Society.

www.xulonpress.com

April, 2011

For our guest,
 Ben Kononoff!
May this book help some christians to respond effectively when challenged about their faith.
May it also cause some non-christians to re-think their position.
Prov. 3:5-6
 H. G. Stuebe

Purpose and Relevance

The purpose of this book is to address challenges to the Christian faith. It is therefore most meaningful to those who may be struggling in their faith or faced with arguments opposing the Christian faith. Relevance is sought by embedding it in the story of an ordinary family living and working in a small town. The story could be called a study in workplace apologetics since most experiences mentioned in it are at the jobsite but challenges within the family and community are also a major component.

There will be those who recognize similarities between the town, industry or people they know and the people, town and industry in the book. Please do not make undue connections. This story is fiction although the illustrations in Chapter 8 are drawn from the author's own experiences. The implications of the story are true to life.

Group Discussion

Questions about each chapter are included at the end of the story for those who want to use this approach. Most of them are deliberately probing in order to invite discussion. They are best suited to be used in an interactive group that is not hesitant to explore sensitive areas.

Acknowledgements

I am grateful for suggestions from those who read part or all of various editions and revisions of the manuscript. The feedback presented has been useful and much of it incorporated in this edition. This does not mean that all of those listed below agree with the content. It will always be subject to improvements, so the best use of this story is as a catalyst for discussions, revisions and possible applications.

Bill Wiebe	Freda Wiebe	
Fathom Twain	Doug Treadwell	Patrick Pugsley
Bill Powers	Ken Moore	Rocky Moore
Ron Holden	Bill Goetz	Rod Freeman
Charles Cooper	Richard Brooks	Jacquie Bicknell

Table of Contents

Chapter	Title	Page
1	Moving	15
2	Taking a Stand	19
3	Becky Speaks Up	28
4	I'm Talking to You	37
5	Evolution or Creation?	42
6	Dinner with David	46
7	Family Time	50
8	Is God For Real?	54
9	What's All This About Salvation?	65
10	Suspicions Mount	71
11	Gary Opens Up	74
12	Seven Musts of Marriage	80
13	Decisions! Decisions!	87
14	Struggling with Prayer	94
15	The Trap	98
16	Facing Crucial Issues	102
17	More Critical Issues	107
18	Surprises	123
Appendix 1	Three Aspects of Salvation	131
Appendix 2	Guidelines for Learning	133
Appendix 3	Prayer	137
Appendix 4	Worship	141
Appendix 5	Decisions	143
	Questions for each chapter	147

Faith Under Fire

Roy wandered aimlessly from one lonely room to the next while clutching the letter in his hand. This is not the way it was supposed to turn out. This was to have been a venture of faith for the whole family. He was so sure great things were ahead when they moved here, and now this.
"Teresa and I won't be coming home for Thanksgiving, dad. I know it will be hard for you to be alone." That was the opening line of the letter. The din of silence rocked his emotions. Roy walked over to a window and stared at the road that had led the family to this place nearly 10 years ago. In his mind he replayed that scene and the events of the first few months.

Chapter 1

Moving

"Dad, why are we moving here?" asked 12 year old Teresa, in a grumpy way.

"It's like I've said, honey," replied dad. "The drier weather will keep mom healthier. Besides you'll have hot summers and beaches and fruit and even fun in the snow on the mountain nearby. Look at these mountains and lakes and orchards and birds. It's a great place. You'll find friends too."

"I sure hope so," moaned Teresa.

The dad, Roy, knew why Teresa moaned. She had been a popular girl in the school they came from. She did well in just about anything she got into. They had enjoyed many exchanges on topics beyond her years, an exercise he was particularly fond of. She was special to him. He also knew that this move could severely affect their relationship, depending on how she reacted.

"You'll be OK," encouraged Denver, her 14 year old brother, "I'll miss my friends too. We just have to make the best of it for mom."

"Thanks, Denver," replied Becky, the mother, "you *are* a real trooper. I feel bad that I'm the reason you had to move."

"Don't feel that way, mom," responded Denver, "we'll be OK."

Denver's supportive words were particularly meaningful for Becky. They came at a cost for him that she understood better than any others in the family because they both struggled with health issues that limited their social life. She and Roy were grateful that this came from Denver voluntarily because he would likely have the hardest adjustment. It had taken Denver a long time to become accepted in their former location due to his cleft palate operation and resulting facial disfigurement. Now he would have to battle for acceptance again at an age when friends are even more important.

"We're together in this, honey, this move will be good for all of us," declared Roy to his wife.

"I hope so," sighed Becky. Her sigh was more about her concern for Denver than for herself. The two of them shared many deep personal conversations. Becky knew what was at stake here.

Spirits lifted as they circled a small lake near the town and noted the stunning background scene centered on a steep bluff to the north. The early May blossoms were in full bloom in the orchards. All they now needed was to find the right house to buy for a move this summer. Roy already had employment arranged at a local RV manufacturing plant. Tough as the decision had been, he and Becky were convinced the Lord was in it and the days ahead would have God's blessing even if other experiences weren't always pleasant.

A home was found near that very same lake and by summer the whole family was enjoying the benefits of life in their new surroundings. Roy was getting to know some of his fellow-workers at the plant after two months at work and could sense that he was in for a new experience. There were some rough characters there. Somehow he'd have to establish a good relationship without compromising his commitment to the Lord. It would not be easy. Little did he know just how tough it would be.

Denver was increasingly apprehensive about starting school in September among strangers. He had met very few boys his age around their new home since many of the residents were seniors. It did not look good for him. Teresa somehow managed to connect with a few girls in spite of the hurdles. She had always found that easier than Denver. She was already looking forward to the new school.

The first day of school came and went. It didn't take long for a familiar pattern to develop. One day after school a few weeks later Denver was alone at his locker getting ready to go home. Few who walked by even acknowledged his existence. Some made it clear by their actions and expressions that they thought of him as a freak. "Hey, kid! Did you run into a pole with your face?" sneered one bully. "Yah," added his buddy. "Hope you didn't damage the pole." Cruel laughter followed.

Just down the hallway was Teresa's locker and crowded around her were several girls and guys, obviously wanting to get to know her and be her friends. "Why is it like this?" was the anguish that plagued Denver. "It's not fair. I didn't make myself the way I am. I've got feelings too."

Denver walked home feeling down. "What's a 14 year old doing going home to be comforted by momma?" he thought. Engrossed in his inner struggle he stepped into the crosswalk without looking first. "Hey, you! Are you stupid as well as ugly?" snarled the driver as he screeched to a stop. "Wanna get yourself killed?" For a moment that seemed like a better option than what was happening to him, but he apologized, backed up, and dismissed that thought. He was going home to encourage his mom and not to think about himself. He had to get over his discouragement before he reached home. His mom needed him.

Becky's physical health improved at least slightly over the next months. Friendships were formed at a local evangelical church and things were looking up for the family, even though it was harder for Denver. It looked like the Lord was definitely in this move, their faith was being rewarded. Now that confidence was shattered as Roy read the next lines in the letter...again.

"It's not like we're planning some kind of payback for being so focused on your testimony at work while ignoring us at home or making other kids shun us because of your reputation at work. But it's true that we have other plans just like I often felt you had other plans that didn't include us." Roy cringed as he recalled his first encounter at work that led to those time-consuming commitments Denver referred to.

Chapter 2

Taking a Stand

"Hey, Roy," yelled Jeb as the men in his crew gathered for lunch, "you didn't laugh at my joke."

"You're right, I didn't."

"Whatsa matter, not clean enough for you? Didn't like me making fun of Jesus, did you?"

"Guess not."

"So what are you gonna do? Preach at us and make us all into nice goodie-goodies?" laughed Jim, a buddy of Jeb's.

"What makes you think I would do that?" asked Roy.

"I see that you pray before you eat. Probably putting in a word for us poor sinners too. Well, it ain't gonna work on me. I had that stuff shoved down my throat as a kid and I hated everything about it!" stormed Jeb. "Nobody's gonna drag me into believin' any of this Jesus baloney!" (Vulgarities omitted)

"Cool it, Jeb," interjected Sam, "he hasn't done anything like that to us."

"What have you got against Jesus, Jeb?" ventured Roy.

"He figured he was the only way. He figured he was God. Everybody has to follow him. Why should we be loyal to a God who set us up in a world we didn't ask for? If he's so smart why is this world in such a mess. There's just a whole bunch of idiots all thinking he is the answer. What arrogance! " (Vulgarities omitted)

"Who was he then?"

"He was a nutcase who duped a lot of people but he's not fooling me. A whole bunch of weak and wimpy idiots are being sucked in."

"That's not how I see it," responded Roy. "He's the best friend I've got. I don't think you'd like it if I talked about your friend the way you talked about Jesus. So that's why I didn't laugh at your joke."

A few more mutterings and muffled comments ended that topic as they all headed back to work.

Several days later Jeb called out to Roy in the middle of lunch-time. "Been out fishing with you best friend lately, Roy?"

"Depends on what kind of fish, Jeb."

"Ya, I get it. Like when they taught us "I will make you fishers of men" in that Sunday School, right? What a bunch of crap! They were lunatics just like this Jesus of yours." (Vulgarities omitted)

"That is one of the choices we can make about who Jesus was. I could show you some other conclusions. You've made your viewpoint clear several times so maybe I should be able to present mine. Fair play, right?"

The men around Roy muttered a bit and a few agreed.

"Suppose I draw this square in the dirt and divide it into 4 sections. At the top I'll put the question: Was Jesus actually God in human form? Then I'll put the answer NO at the top of the first column and YES at the top of the other column. On the left I'll put the question: Did Jesus claim to be God? Then I'll put the answer NO in front of the top row and YES for the bottom row."

Some of the guys drifted off in disgust but a few gathered closer to Roy to see what this was all about. Jeb was one of the ones who stayed. The result was something like the box shown here.

Was Jesus actually God in human form?

		NO	YES
Did Jesus claim to be God?	NO	1.	3.
	YES	2.	4.

"This set-up allows four possible answers. Makes sense?"

There were some half-hearted nods of agreement. Another guy moved off into the fringe of the circle and ignored Roy, but a few others gave Roy their attention, so he continued. "Here's the scoop.

1. If Jesus was not God and did not claim to be God he is just a fairy-tale legend that has ballooned into absurd claims, so we'll put LEGEND in the top left box.
2. If he was not God but claimed to be God he is a lunatic just like Jeb said or like I would be if I claimed to be Abraham Lincoln. So LUNATIC goes into the bottom left box.
3. If he really was God but claimed he was not then he would be a liar. Top right box gets LIAR.
4. If he really was God and also declared that he was God then he is the Lord. The bottom right box gets LORD.

This is then what the box would look like when filled in.

Was Jesus actually God in human form?

		NO	YES
Did Jesus claim to be God?	NO	1. LEGEND	3. LIAR
	YES	2. LUNATIC	4. LORD

Is that logical?" concluded Roy.

The men looked at the diagram etched into the dirt.

Sam replied, speaking for the group, "Looks like it has to be one of the four but not necessarily the one you would choose."

"We all have to make our own decision," concluded Roy. "We all have a choice about which one we'll believe."

At this point it was time to get back to work but it was clear that Jeb was seething with anger. On the way to the work station he "accidentally" kicked Roy's tool box, spilling the contents onto the floor. Roy wondered what this would come to.

During the afternoon break Jeb went over to Roy and challenged him. Obviously something had been churning inside him all afternoon.

"You're basing everything on what the Bible says," argued Jeb. "That's the whole problem you Christians have. The Bible is just another collection of something some wise guys wrote, yet you are basing your whole life on it and dumping it on us. You expect me to swallow that garbage?" (Vulgarities omitted)

"You've hit the nail right on the head, Jeb, that is the fundamental question," responded Roy. "Why would I trust the Bible? Most people ignore or reject it. I can tell you why I believe in it even though most people do not agree with me. By faith believers are counting on it to be true. On the other hand, also by faith those who don't believe it are counting on it not to be true. So would you give me a chance to tell you why I do trust it, since you've challenged me rather bluntly?"

"Well, OK. You're on but you won't convince me," grunted Jeb. "Make it short." The two of them sat down off to one side and Roy breathed a silent prayer before beginning. A few of the other men sauntered over just close enough to be in on it. One of them was a fellow named Harry.

"Any book, writing, or system of belief that claims to be from God **MUST be able to fulfill at least three criteria,**" continued Roy. "Here are the three that I think count the most.

1. The ideas and principles it teaches **must ring true** to life. They must match reality and therefore actually work. Every day we believe in things that work, like remote controls, telephones, and computers even if we don't understand them. We even believe in them if sometimes they don't work. For the Bible to be true its principles must work, or ring true all the time.
2. Any predictions it makes **must come true** 100% of the time if it is God's Word. Nine out of ten doesn't cut it. This is called prophecy of the future and there are many in the Bible.
3. It has to be able to transform lives and **make them true**. No matter which age group, culture, status, period of time or location on earth it must have the power to change lives. The Bible does that.

Note that it has to measure up to all three criteria. Just doing one or two of them won't do. I believe that the Bible is the only book that does all three."

Jeb argued, "You may believe that but I sure don't and neither do most sane people."

"You have that choice," conceded Roy.

"And I believe in getting to work," demanded the foreman, Gary, who had shown up in the background. "You're both late. We're not here to discuss religion. Let's go."

"You are right, sir," responded Roy. "My apologies. I'll be more careful about the time in the future. How about I stay for half an hour longer to make up for both of us since I'm at fault. I can do some clean-up work that doesn't need the assembly line."

Jeb was a bit surprised and so was Gary.

"What," queried Gary, "you'd do what?"

"I'll stay for an extra half-hour," answered Roy. "Would that make up for my mistake?"

"Well, OK, if that's what you want," mumbled Gary.

When the rest had left at the end of the day Harry stayed to work with Roy for part of the time because he had a question. He was not the type to ask questions publicly.

"I've talked to a lot of people about religions and faiths and philosophies," ventured Harry. "The most reasonable conclusion I can come to is that Jesus was the son of a Roman soldier who had an affair with Mary. Jesus managed to teach a lot of things that were true but his accomplishments were exaggerated by his followers. Those stories of miracles are embellishments of history. So, in that diagram you made I believe he is an ordinary human being who became a legend."

"That is a conclusion many come to but it is not the conclusion that the Bible gives," replied Roy. "Who you believe he is becomes your choice. Just recognize that it has to make sense. Saying that he was a good man who became a legend due to over-zealous followers leaves a lot of questions. His most devoted followers fled, abandoned him and locked themselves away out of fear when he was crucified. What transformed them into bold, passionate missionaries? They were willing to lay down their lives for him. People aren't willing to do that for a fairy tale. It was the resurrection he had promised that did it. They saw him a number of times after he had been in the sealed tomb guarded by Roman soldiers who were to keep the tomb secure upon pain of death. He came back to life anyway. Legends don't come back to life like that. The Son of God does."

"So you are saying that Jesus really was who he claimed to be and who his disciples proclaimed him to be," responded Harry.

"Right."

"I've got to think that one over some more," pondered Harry, thoughtfully. Roy wasn't sure what to think as he saw Harry leaving. On the one hand there was this sense of euphoria. What he had so much hoped would be his opportunity to share the gospel seemed to be coming together! He could hardly contain the excitement! On the other hand, was he just causing trouble and creating enemies? What was all this going to turn into? He could hardly wait to get home and share news of the event with his family.

Roy had phoned home to say that he would be at least half and hour late and would explain. This he did at the supper table with Denver and Teresa there too. In spite of the anger of some and the reprimand from the foreman, Roy painted an enthusiastic picture of the joy in taking a stand for the Lord. He urged the family to pray for all those involved and for him to have the wisdom to handle the situation correctly. Roy became totally absorbed in what to do next. Teresa started to talk about some challenges to faith that she was encountering at school but Roy told her just to stand firm. He would talk to her about it later when he had more time. The probing talks he used to have with her didn't seem to be the priority right now. Denver timidly alluded to rebuffs and mistreatments he encountered at school but it almost seemed as though Roy didn't notice the hurt that needed attention from him. He was so pre-occupied about developments at work that Becky had to speak to him three times before she got his attention. Denver again wanted to ask him about something that was bothering him but Roy remembered the evangelism planning meeting at the church that evening. That would be just the right place to share developments that had taken place at work. He had to leave right away but told Denver he'd get back to him later. Later didn't happen.

After Roy was gone Becky approached Denver to ask him what it was that had been troubling him. Denver was reluctant to respond but finally blurted out, "After school a bunch of guys ganged up on me and were bullying me and threatening to beat me up."

"That's awful, what happened?"

"Just then Teresa and a few of her friends came around the corner and saw what was happening. She really lit into them, called them cowards for ganging up four against one. She yelled at them and challenged them to take on a little girl to show how brave they were. The guys were shocked."

"What did those bullies do?"

"They didn't seem to know what to do, so they made some jokes about a little sister having to protect her older brother. Then they made some comments about me that I won't repeat and left. Teresa did a really brave thing but where does this leave me?"

"Denver, I'm so sorry this has happened. We've got to find a way to deal with this. We won't leave you alone in this."

The next lines in the letter really hurt. "Mom tried to get you to understand what was happening. You needed to show that you cared about us too. We needed quality family time. She was so patient and understanding with all of us. There was one period of time when you did what she suggested and I appreciate that. You showed that you cared for those two years and it helped. In the end I still had to deal with some inner struggles myself. I guess that is not your fault."Again Roy recalled the scene.

Chapter 3

Becky Speaks Up

Roy had sensed that neither one of the children were as excited about this turn of events as he was, but he accepted that as normal for children that age. Later that evening when the two of them were alone Becky added another perspective.

"Roy, did you notice some apprehension in Denver and Teresa when you told them about today's adventures?" asked Becky.

"Yes, I did, but isn't that normal for children that age?"

"Maybe", continued Becky, "but I wonder if it goes deeper than that."

"What else could it be?" asked Roy.

At this point Becky told Roy about Denver's predicament and how he had wanted to talk to his dad about it. Roy was heartbroken over what he had done.

"There's more, Roy," Becky continued. "It could be that some of their classmates have a dad who works where you do and stories get around. Those classmates could end up resenting our kids when they hear the story from their dads. It may also be that they are starting to wonder if the men at work are more important to you than your own children.

When were you last excited about something they were doing?"

"Ouch! You've put your finger on a sore spot, Becky. What would you suggest I do?"

"You've got to talk to Denver and let him know that you care. Also, the school is putting on a concert soon. Teresa is in the band. We need to be there and make a special attempt to acknowledge her part in it. Denver is likely to make the soccer team for the school and he really needs us to be there when he plays. What's the chance of getting some time off late one afternoon to be at the game?"

"Well, good suggestions. I'll go see Denver and we can sure be at the concert. The soccer game could be a problem if starts too early. Perhaps I can rush over from work and get in the last half. When is the game?"

"I'll get the details. Meanwhile, show an interest by asking them about these things. It says something that you didn't know about these matters without me telling you. Talk to them about their lives, Roy."

"Yes, you're right. I'll do that."

Roy did spend time with Denver to repair the relationship and work on a plan for Denver to help him overcome his predicament. He promised to be there for him in whatever way would help. The key problem for Denver was that he felt like a good for nothing reject. The opportunity for Roy to act on the other suggestions came the next day at supper.

"Hey, Denver, I hear that you're trying out for the soccer team. How's it going?"

"It's tough, dad. I'm new and it looks like the coach has his eye on guys that have been there a while. Unless I'm much better than they, I don't think I'll get picked," murmured Denver.

"That's rough, Denver. I remember what it was like the times I wasn't chosen."

"You mean you lost out sometimes too?"

"Oh, yes. It felt like the end of the world at the time. You begin to look at yourself as a failure."

"But you were good at some things, dad. I'm not good at anything."

"You are good at something, very good! In spite of what happens to you I see you as a kindhearted and caring person. That's worth more than a spot on a soccer team. What do you say you just give it your best. You're a winner just for trying even if the other guy is chosen. Let me know how it goes, OK?"

"OK, dad."

"Do I hear that you are in a concert coming up, Teresa?"

"Yep, I'm one of the youngest ones chosen to play in the band. They usually choose only from Grades 9 and up but the band leader said I'm doing so well on the clarinet that he'll let me try. Isn't that great, dad!"

"Good for you, Teresa," exclaimed Roy. "We'll be there to listen. When is the concert?"

"It'll be two weeks from Friday night and I need to practice some more right after supper."

Roy couldn't help but see the downcast look on Denver's face. Such a contrast to Teresa's.

The whole family was at the concert, but Denver was not chosen for the team. The look of dejection on his face during the concert told the story. For him it was another failure, another rejection, another winner for Teresa and a loser for him. He so much needed affirmation and Becky was determined to make up for it in whatever way she could. But how would she do that? Roy needed to be there for him too.

At home that evening Becky broached the subject with Roy.

"Honey, did you notice Denver's face during the concert?" queried Becky.

"Yes, I did. He was not a happy camper. Must be because Teresa is experiencing success and fulfillment but he is getting the shaft."

"We've got to do something, Roy. I think you need to act now."

"What if I took him out for breakfast and then the two of us could spend the day canoeing and fishing and hiking or whatever? It's Saturday tomorrow and the weather is looking good enough for that. I'll just surprise him with the idea in the morning."

"Great idea, hon. Go for it!"

Very early the next morning Roy knocked on Denver's door. Sitting on the edge of his bed Roy said, "Denver, I'd like to load up the canoe and some fishing gear, go out for breakfast and just get out there for the day. But I don't want to go alone. I'd like you to come with me. What do you say?"

"Me," exclaimed Denver with surprise! "Really?"

"Yep."

"Sure thing, dad. I'll be ready in minutes!"

With the canoe firmly on the rack and a hearty breakfast in their tummies the two of them headed for a popular fishing lake not far away. Although the weather had begun to turn cool it was still a very decent day for what Roy had in mind. The cool weather actually improved the fishing prospects. They hiked some trails, chatted about life in general and then found a suitable place for a campfire to heat up the lunch Becky had prepared plus adding their fish to the menu.

"Denver," Roy began, "I sense that school is not a thrilling experience for you yet. You don't have to talk about it if you don't want to. I don't want to spoil the day but if you care to chat about it I'm here for you."

Denver was quiet for a while. Then he opened up to what had been eating away at him for weeks.

"Why is it that most of the others have friends, are good at something and have fun while I don't get any of that? I'm just a nobody at school. Why did God make me like this?"

"You're important to us, Denver. We love you and you mean a lot to us. God has a very important place for you in life just the way you are. We want you to discover that and enjoy life too. You are really good at some things, especially the way you encourage mom. You've been a real trooper there. Now, how can we help you?"

"Mom is already helping a lot. Without her there I'd be in a lot more trouble. She really tries to encourage me."

"I guess you're also saying that I haven't been there for you like I ought."

"You're busy with so many other things – work, church, your friends, stuff around the house. Sometimes I feel that I don't count for much but I know that you need to do those things. I just don't know what to think. I just have to fight my own battles."

"Denver, we could fight them together. I've got an idea. Let's you and I do things like this more often and keep in touch about what is happening in your life. But we also need to just have fun together. There have got to be places to go and things to do that we don't even know about. Once in a while, if you want to, you can invite a guy to come along. What do you say?"

"That sounds good, dad! I'm feeling better already."

"Hey, Denver, see that peak over there? Think we can make it?"

"Why not? I'm game!"

The two finished lunch, got a bit more fishing in and hiking done and then headed home in great spirits. It was a really good day. Roy felt he had gained a better perspective on his responsibilities. Things would be better from now on.

The letter continued. "I was really thrilled when you suggested that we go exploring, hiking, fishing and canoeing together. I looked forward to those times. But somehow it didn't get me to the place where I knew why I even existed. Sometimes other issues were more important for you." Roy grimaced with pain as he recalled a specific example.

"Hey Roy! Wait up," called Sam as he spotted him half a block away in town the next Saturday.
"Oh, hi Sam," responded Roy. "How you doin'?"
"Fine, fine, Roy. Got time for a coffee?"
"Sure, how about the coffee shop just up ahead?"
"Works for me, Roy. It's my treat. Let's go."

When the niceties of social interaction were out of the way, Sam came out with the reason he called Roy. He was a bit hesitant to approach the subject but there was a sense of determination about the way he presented it.
"Roy, I can't help but admire the stand you took with the guys at work a few days ago even though I don't believe you are right. It has created a bit of a dilemma for me. I feel as though I have to let you know where I'm at so that there are no misunderstandings because I'm afraid this could build into something unpleasant."
"Do you feel that I'm a troublemaker?" asked Roy.
"Well, no and yes, I suppose. You're not a troublemaker because what you stand for is largely wholesome, but some guys will take offense big time if they feel pushed."
"Are you saying that I should hold off and keep the peace?"
"Not quite. After all, you didn't start the debate. You responded when you were challenged and that was a wise and legitimate move. What I'd like to suggest is that you take a good look at your own convictions and see if they really are worth fighting for."

"Do you really know what my convictions are?" asked Roy.

"I've studied philosophy, religion, and psychology as well as learning how to read people. You are a conservative, evangelical, somewhat fundamental Christian and I think I know what you stand for," countered Sam.

Roy had to admit to himself that Sam had him pretty well taped. Roy winced a little and adjusted his seating a bit in his discomfort.

"OK, Sam, I see you're pretty astute. I'll give you that one. You probably have some specific things you want me to think about. Might as well lay them out. I'll listen."

"Thanks, Roy. I appreciate your attitude and I'll try to be respectful when I say this but I know that I tend to get pretty vehement about some issues so be prepared."

"Alright, shoot."

"I'll limit myself to three issues, even though there are more. One is your conviction that the Bible is God's Word from cover to cover. Are you aware of the Council of Nicene that assembled to decide which writings belonged in the canon of the New Testament and which did not? I don't know how that Old Testament was put together but some guy or group must have edited that one too. These are just human documents that some group has awarded the reputation of being God's Word and you've swallowed the story."

"That's like giving me both barrels, Sam. I regret that I invited you to shoot."

They both laughed a bit, which eased the tension.

Roy continued. "My answer to that is the same as I gave Jeb, which you may have heard. I could add some other things too but I promised to listen."

"My second issue," declared Sam, "is the concept of hell that you preach in your church. How can a God who says he is love invent a place of torment like that? You claim that he is a perfect Being that knows the end from the beginning. If he's perfect how come what he created is such a failure? And if he knows the future why did he make people anyway? It's a travesty! A cruel joke. How can it be justice when the penalty far exceeds any wrong the person has done? I don't believe in hell!"

"I can understand a bit about how you feel," answered Roy. "Carry on."

"My third beef is the arrogance you conservative Christians have in thinking that your religion is the only truth. There is much we can learn from many different religions and there is much we need to reject in each one of them including Christianity. I strenuously object to anyone who claims to have all the answers or to be The Truth!" Sam began to get fairly worked up at this point, and decided to stop there before drawing the attention of everyone else in the restaurant.

"Let me give some thought to those three things, Sam," offered Roy. "Then I can get back to you. May I ask why you have spent so much time studying Christianity when you don't believe in it?"

"I was a Bible school student for two years long ago. I turned against it. But you don't need to get back to me or discuss theology with me. Just remember the cautions I suggest," retorted Sam.

With that the two men finished their coffee in a somewhat tense mood and then parted. There was turmoil in Roy's heart and mind as he tried to figure out how he would answer Sam.

Roy went home troubled. It was one thing to be opposed by an angry rebel, but quite another to get opposition from a knowledgeable, but respectful, opponent who had been to Bible school. At home the family could tell that his mind was somewhere else. Becky tried to draw Roy out of his troubled state without much success. She could tell that there was an inner struggle going on that he wasn't ready to talk about. Perhaps he thought it would make him look weak. Denver wanted to do something with dad that Saturday afternoon but gave up the attempt. Teresa drifted to the periphery and became absorbed in one of her own rewarding pursuits. Things were not going as Becky had hoped. Now what?

Denver's letter had made it clear to Roy that the so-called "significant events at work" weren't without a down side. He had become so engrossed with the issues that it was sucking the life out of him. It wasn't hard for him to think of a few more examples. Roy chafed within himself. Wasn't there a positive side to it as well? Aren't we supposed to "... stand firm, let nothing move you, always give yourself fully to the work of the Lord..." 1 Cor. 15:58? Roy thought of the time when the 'for' and 'against' groups began to identify themselves.

Chapter 4

I'm Talking to You

For the next few days the whole group avoided 'religious' talk. Roy wasn't eager about getting into any debates. Sam kept the reins on the others somehow. He seemed to have been granted informal leadership in the crew by common consent. However, some events Sam couldn't stop made it clear that Roy had made a few mild enemies. His tools were misplaced, staples from staple guns 'accidentally' hit him and snide remarks peppered the conversation in the work area. Roy didn't react to these and kept up his practice of giving thanks at mealtime anyway. The group neither acknowledged nor ridiculed it. However, it was obvious that Jeb was disturbed. Finally one day he vented his concern, something Roy secretly hoped wouldn't happen.

"Roy, remember your talk about proof of who Jesus is? Well, it falls flat," declared Jeb. "If he is who he claims to be then why hasn't he told everyone? How could he hold them responsible? That's a raw deal. Your story is full of holes." (Vulgarities omitted)

Roy couldn't duck that one, even though there was something in him that just didn't want to debate with Jeb. He pondered the question, flung a brief prayer heavenward and spoke.

"You are right that many have not heard of Jesus but that doesn't mean that God hasn't communicated with them," answered Roy. "He has ways of getting through to people that we may not realize."

"Are you trying to tell me that God has been talking to everyone on earth including me?"

"Yes."

"That's a bunch of baloney!"

"No, there are at least three ways that he talks to everyone on earth, including you. He's telling us things about himself loud and clear.

1. How did all these complex and wonderful things we see in nature get here? I hear that Harry here is a superb woodworker, making beautiful things out of wood. Suppose I went to his place and marveled at how all those crafty things managed to get there without somebody designing and making them? They just got there by themselves. That would be the height of insult! This world is full of an enormous number of plants, animals and systems incredibly more complex than any woodwork. There is a Designer and Owner of all that exists. He is way above and beyond us. We know there is a God, a Creator. Creation speaks loudly to us."

"Haven't you heard of the Big Bang, Roy?" asked Jim. "That started everything off and evolution did the rest."

"Lots of people believe that. I don't," answered Roy. "What was it that went Bang if everything that exists emerged after the Bang? To believe that nothingness condensed into one spot and then decided to explode forming all the stars, planets and eventually everything that exists is a bigger fairytale than all others put together. Do you really believe that?"

There was mumbling and grumbling but no discernable answer so Roy continued.

"Here's the second way God speaks to us.

2. The circumstances that happen to us like problems, catastrophes, failures and death make us think. It seems many people don't ever consider God unless they are in deep trouble. These events speak to us.
    "So, when the thunder and lightning hits my house God is judging me, eh?" snarled Jeb.
    "Not necessarily, Jeb, but it will make us think. Here's the third one.

3. Our conscience reminds us that there is such a thing as right and wrong. This can only be if we are morally accountable to Someone higher up. We know there is a standard. If everything just came by accident there can be no such thing as right and wrong."

Sam interjected at this point. "Morality is an artificial construction we have devised ourselves. We make our own laws as a community of people. There are no absolute truths."

"That's definitely how many people think but not what the Bible teaches. Romans chapter one makes it clear that we do have a moral accountability built in to us that renders every person without excuse. There are another three that make many of us even more accountable."

"Hogwash!" stormed Jeb. "Evolution has proven that there is no Creator, nobody is manipulating events to try to get to us and when we die it's all over. There's nobody there to take us to no court or whatever!" (Vulgarities omitted)

"Let him finish, Jeb. He says he's got three more points." interrupted Sam. "Give the guy a chance to present his case. I don't agree with all he says but I will listen."

Jeb mumbled some objections but Roy continued, "The other three ways God communicates with us involve Scripture, making the hearer that much more accountable.

4. The commands and explanations we read in the Bible are like God talking to us.
5. Jesus coming to earth gives tangible evidence that God cares about us. What we learn about the person of Christ who has promised to be with those who trust him deepens our understanding and gives a personal touch to the relationship.
6. Last, what he did for us on the cross speaks volumes.

It helps me to remember them if I think of them as the 6 C's: creation, circumstances, conscience, commands, Christ and the cross. These render mankind completely responsible for spiritual decisions. We can't really claim that no one has ever heard."

"Rubbish," argued Jeb! "There's no one up there who cares about us or what happens to us. If there was he'd do something about the mess this planet is in. It's all just garbage."

Several of the men made their displeasure with Roy obvious later on. There were snide remarks, pranks played on his tools and even cases of disruption to his work. Sam saw it and came over to Roy to help him straighten things out.

"This is absolutely disgusting!" stormed Sam. "I'm going to let them know how immature and idiotic this is even though I disagree with you."

Roy didn't know what to say. He was glad Sam was helpful but at a loss of what to say or do himself. At the beginning of the next break Sam kept his word and spoke up.

"Guys," he said, "I helped Roy get his tools back together and straighten out the mess someone made of the job he was doing. I think this is disgustingly immature behavior by someone here. I will not just stand by. This ends right here and now or else!"

There was some grumbling and mumbling but they all knew Sam meant it and knew how to follow through on his threat. No one admitted doing it but it didn't happen again. Nor did anyone start any further debate that day.

However, several of the men were intrigued by the answers they heard earlier from Roy. Tom and Harry approached Roy later in the afternoon when others weren't around and asked if he would be willing to meet once a week with the two of them in the evening to privately pursue these discussions in depth. Roy agreed to a Thursday evening. At home that night he shared his sense of joy over what was developing. Becky said she would help set things up for the Thursday nights. Denver and Teresa were noncommittal. In the weekly Tuesday Small Group meeting associated with the church that he and Becky were part of, they shared what was happening and gained support in prayer. The church's prayer chain was mobilized too. Roy eagerly looked forward to his time with the two men. Dividing lines were being drawn. What next?

*That **was** significant, Denver," argued Roy in his thoughts. "It's not fair to dump all that as just a hindrance to our family! Didn't you notice what it did for Tom and Harry?"*

Chapter 5

Evolution or Creation?

At their first meeting with Roy, both Tom and Harry came with one question foremost in their minds. After some informal chit-chat around coffee and goodies they came to the point.

"Roy," Tom ventured, "we respect the conviction with which you responded to the challenge a few days ago, but we are hung up on this bit about creation and God being interested in people. Looking around it just doesn't seem to be that way. Those guys at work made some passionate statements about the whole issue. Jeb's comment about evolution has merit. Scientists tell us that what we've got on planet earth wasn't created, it just evolved. I've also heard some say that science without religion is sterile, but religion without science is blind. Maybe there was a God who kick-started the process but he sure doesn't seem to be around to manage it. The claims of evolution seem to fit better than what the Bible claims is creation."

"I guess the majority of the world sees it the way you do, Tom," said Roy. "But as for evidence and logic to support either creation or evolution, I place my confidence in creation by a long way. In fact, I would go so far as to say that evolution is not even possible."

"How did you reach that conclusion?" asked Harry.

"From what I have read and studied and thought about seriously, I've come to the conclusion that there are at least six reasons why evolution could not be the answer," responded Roy. "Shall I give them to you?"

"Sure, that's why we're here."

"OK, here goes.

Intelligent Design

Even an item as simple as an arrowhead is accepted as conclusive evidence of formation by design. It was made by someone for a purpose. Our universe from the tiniest cell to the immense outer galaxies is full of intricate systems and complicated organization. How can we conclude there was no designer behind it but there was for the arrowhead? There are theistic evolutionists who would say that God got it started, but then God left the scene and let evolution take over. It's good that they acknowledge God but there's more information that puts the theory of evolution into big trouble. Even a kick-started world cannot evolve into what we have today. Here are some of the reasons why.

Irreducible Complexity

Not only are all cells and organs very complex but they have to be complete all at once in order to function. Part of an organ or part of a system doesn't make an animal or a plant fit for survival. It makes it worse! The idea of hanging on to the beginnings of an eye until after millions of years the optic nerves and receptor brain cells just happen to develop to match it is preposterous. The same is true of any feature for any plant or animal. Not only that, in most of the animal and plant world a matching male – female pair is needed right away or the species doesn't survive. This has to be repeated millions and millions of times in plants and animals, all by chance if evolution is to be true. Not possible!

DNA and Mutations

The DNA of a human being contains the programmed instructions for its development. It is estimated that these instructions would fill a 500 volume encyclopedia. When the cell splits to form two, a copy of the instructions is made. This process produces not millions, not billions but trillions of cells each with a copy. Darwin thought that the cell was simple. We now know it was far from simple.

Mutations occur when parts of the instructions in the DNA are **lost** or **inaccurate**. This results in degeneration not in improvements. In order for one organism to change to a different species there would have to be the **addition** of DNA instructions. The whole blueprint would then have to be rewritten to match. That simply does not happen. Mutations don't do that, and therefore cannot produce a new species. Organisms reproduce **after their kind** with variety occurring within the species.

Moral Accountability

The whole human race has a built-in sense of moral responsibility. This did not accidentally develop from an inanimate piece of matter but from the image of God planted in mankind by the Creator. He has clear standards about what he wants from us and will hold us responsible. Without this accountability there can't even be such a thing as right and wrong.

Second Law of Thermodynamics

This law states that the entropy of a closed system tends to a maximum. It means that anything left to itself will become more random and chaotic, not more complex or organized. This is the opposite of what the theory of evolution proposes.

First Cause

Both the theories of creation and evolution are faced with the question of what they start with. We either accept an eternally self-existing God capable of designing the universe or an eternally self-existing piece of matter capable of evolving into our universe. If we reject both of those we are faced with the idea that if you start with nothing and wait long enough than by chance mutations and natural selection you will get everything. That would be truly ridiculous."

The three of them spent the rest of the evening hashing through the implications of the above. In the end they concluded that both camps accept what they believe in by faith since neither one can reproduce an observable sequence to prove the position. Creationists by faith count on what the Bible teaches to be true, and evolutionists by faith count on it not to be true, each claiming evidence for their convictions. The choice is with the individual. Tom and Harry left with lots to think about. Roy stayed home with lots to pray about. Now what? A very different turn of events was about to unfold.

"You are right about one thing, Denver" thought Roy. "I did get almost obsessed with the issues that came up." This near-obsession was about to take a serious turn.

Chapter 6

Dinner with David

A few weeks later, just as quitting time approached, Roy was beckoned over by a man he had seen before but never really met. He introduced himself as David Tyler, Sales Manager in the company. He asked Roy if he could set up a dinner appointment with him sometime during the week. He'd explain what it was about when they got together.

Roy was puzzled but agreed to the offer.

They met a few days later in a local restaurant and spent the first while getting to know one another.

"I was transferred here by the company a few years ago. It's a great place to live. I like it here and the job's going well too," offered David.

"Well, we moved here because my wife needed a better climate for her health's sake. I believe it was the right move, and, yes, I really like it here too," responded Roy.

"Is your family fitting into the community OK?" asked David.

"For the most part, yes. Our son, Denver, is having a more difficult time than the rest but on the whole it is going OK. Being part of a local church family has helped a lot."

"We belong to the church up on the hill that you can see through the window. We attend pretty regularly. It's good to be part of something like that," offered David. "I hear that you've been getting into some intense debates with some of the crew during lunch or breaks."

"Yes, that's true. I didn't start them, but I didn't hold back from answering their questions either. Has someone been complaining to you about me?"

"Sort of, maybe. It's just that I've heard talk about the altercations. We believe it is in the best interests of the company if the workers get along well. This brings me to the reason why we are meeting. I promised to tell you, didn't I? The short version is that we respect the right of people to have their religious convictions, but not to preach them at work. We've found that religion and politics are just too controversial to be on the agenda with the guys. Business is business and I don't bring Christian principles into it or foist them on others. I suggest you do the same."

"Is this an order from the management?" asked Roy.

"No, it's just personal advice so that neither you nor others get hurt. Let's keep things calm."

"I really don't know how that is going to turn out," responded Roy. "If someone asks a question or challenges me am I supposed to say nothing?"

"Why not just tell them you'll think about it and get back to them privately?"

"That could sound like I'm wiggling out of it."

"Well, whatever you do, we've got to tone things down a lot. The company can't afford trouble."

"I will consider what you say but I can't see how I can promise anything."

"Think about it seriously, Roy," warned David.

With that the two finished dinner and went home.

"What's wrong, Roy?" Becky asked as soon as he walked in. She could tell that he was disturbed about something.

"This dinner with David didn't turn out to be what I expected," replied Roy. "He's connected to that church up on the hill but wants me to stay away from discussing religion at work. I know that's a theologically liberal group but what he's doing is advocating a situation where you keep your faith to yourself and to Sunday morning. The rest of the week means business is business and biblical principles don't apply. How can anyone live like that?"

"Have you been muzzled by company decree?"

"No, he's just giving personal advice, supposedly for my own good. Why would he do that when he hasn't even been there for any of our discussions? Why would someone inform the Sales Manager about this kind of an issue? That's a matter for the Personnel Department. I think there's something fishy here."

"So you're getting opposition from all angles. Must mean you're doing something right."

"Dad," interjected Denver, "is that man's name Mr. Tyler?"

"Yes, son, it is but why do you ask?"

"Alex Tyler was beginning to be my friend but the other day he told me he didn't want to see me anymore 'cause my dad was a troublemaker at the RV plant."

Roy and Becky looked at each other in astonishment. The price of standing up for the Lord was beginning to mount and affect the family. The very thing Denver needed, and they had been praying about, was being taken away from him.

"That's awful, Denver, but that accusation is not true. I'm simply answering questions the guys are asking at work and a few don't like my answers. I had no idea it would affect you. I wish I could fix it for you."

"It's not your fault, dad."

Roy lay awake that night for a long time wondering what would be the right move now. It would have to be the Lord stepping in to make a difference. One thing certain was that he needed to give more of his attention to his family. He hadn't realized the impact his witnessing had made on them, or what it had cost them. Roy did spend the next evening just talking about it to Denver.

The letter continued.
"I don't want to be unfair about this, dad. We did have some good times as a family. You did set aside time for me when the chips were down. Those were the times when I felt as though I mattered to you. I know that mom really appreciated them too." Roy remembered how Becky's urging brought about some special family times and restoration of Roy's relationship to his family.

Chapter 7

Family Time

"Becky, Denver and Teresa," began Roy, "I have a proposal to make."

The family stopped eating and glanced apprehensively at Roy across the breakfast table.

"What would you choose if I said that we were going to spend a weekend away together, just the four of us. We'd leave Friday after school and work, then come back Sunday evening. What would you choose to do?"

The family was somewhat taken aback. They had never done this before. Church had always been too important to go away for a whole weekend! This was new!

"Are we camping, staying with relatives or moteling it?" asked Becky.

"You are choosing," replied Roy.

"I vote for camping," declared Denver. "We could rent a small motor home."

"Could I bring a friend?" asked Teresa.

"This is family only, Teresa," ruled Roy. "We need to spend time together as a family so I really think staying with relatives is out too. Where would you want to camp, Denver?"

"I've heard kids talk about a big hydro dam and a real neat Bavarian-type town down across the border. They are only a few hours away. The tours at the dam and their night time laser show are supposed to be really good."

"Sounds good," said Becky. "We could go to one or both depending on how things go. No need to push it if what we're after is time alone together."

"What do you think, Teresa?" asked Roy.

"OK, I guess."

"Then it's settled. Each one will set aside what you need to bring along by Thursday night. I'll see that the motor home is here after work and mom will pack some food, but only some because we will go out for a meal at least once each day. We'll head out and let it take us where we wish, even to the point of changing plans. That would be a new idea for me."

"Yes, that would be a new idea for an organizer like you," agreed Becky.

"Awright, kids! Let's go for it!" exclaimed Roy.

The stuff got packed into the RV, the border crossing was uneventful and the open road was ahead. Occasional stops along the way allowed for short treks, stretch breaks and exploring scenic sites. A campsite had been reserved near the hydro dam, the weather was great and they were even able to have the fish for supper caught by Denver at one of the stops along the way. Table games filled the time after supper while they waited for enough darkness to make the laser show possible. This spectacular light show danced across the 13 acres of spillway as they allowed just enough water to flow to make it a useable screen. The history of the area and the story of the dam's construction fascinated them all.

On Saturday they were able to descend to the inside of the dam on a tour of its inner workings, especially the electricity generating turbines. The gem show in one of the rooms contained a surprising array of crystals and minerals, some they would never have seen otherwise. During the day they explored the region around, hiked a bit and just simply had fun together. That night Roy was very pleased with the way things were going. It took his mind off the stresses that had developed at work. As the family prayed together before going to bed there was genuine joy and thanksgiving for the goodness that God had shown them.

Sunday at breakfast they decided to head for the Bavarian town but not be concerned if they found something more interesting along the way. What Roy found soon after they left wasn't quite what the children had in mind. He spotted a church service about to begin and they pulled into the parking lot to attend just as they were, somewhat reluctantly. Lunch out after that and they were again on their way.

The destination was everything they had been told a Bavarian town might offer. Too soon it was time to head north again, pulling into their own driveway quite late that night.

It had been a good family time. For the next two years Roy concentrated on changing the focus of his priorities. He consistently followed up on his promise to Denver by spending time with him in the evenings and on weekends to work through some of the issues he struggled with. He also purposely planned excursions for just the two of them and sometimes with a friend Denver invited. Some surgical improvements were able to be made on his facial appearance. Some nights were spent helping him with his studies. Mealtimes included open discussions on matters of faith and lifestyle as it affected Denver's and Teresa's lives. Roy cut back somewhat on his responsibilities at the church and restricted his interactions at work to inquirers while maintaining integrity in his testimony. Becky was the recipient of major attention as Roy sought to be a better husband and father. Roy was able to re-connect with Teresa and spent frequent times hashing through issues of life and faith. His family was his first priority in ministry and it was a fulfilling experience. Life seemed to be less stressful during that time but then things changed. At 15 and 17 Teresa and Denver began to get more involved in their own affairs and seemed to desire more independence. Roy and Becky understood this to be normal and they too got involved in their individual pursuits.

The memories of that trip and the wonderful family times of the ensuing two years could not erase the pressure Roy was enduring now that he was all alone at home. Only a miraculous act of God could change the circumstances he was in. The letter in his hand said it all. His whole family was now out of touch with him and he was alone. Over the years Roy had experienced some remarkable interventions from the Lord. He really needed another one now. Couldn't Jesus somehow step into the circumstances and turn it all around? God had done it before. He recalled the time some of the men from work openly challenged him to prove that God had ever been there for him when he needed him. How real was God anyway?

Chapter 8

Is God For Real?

"Hey, Roy. Any fire fall down from heaven for you today?" sneered one worker.

"No, not today." Roy remembered David's warning and wondered if he should sidetrack the conversation, but the two guys wouldn't relent.

"Not today or ever," laughed Jim," 'cause there's nobody up there lighting matches." The men around Jim roared.

"Tell us one example of when God was there for you, Roy. Bet there ain't one," taunted Jeb.

"OK, guys, you asked for it. I'll give you some that I have experienced provided you are willing to listen."

Taken aback a bit by the unexpected turn of events, they grudgingly agreed. They had asked for it. Roy related the following incidents as examples.

Near Suicide

One morning I had this distinct impression that I needed to see a fellow that I had been helping through some difficulties. He had no phone so I drove out to his place that day. I knocked on the door several times without a response. Just as I was in the process of leaving he came to the door. I could tell from the look on his face that he was really depressed.

When he asked what I wanted I just said that I had this inner urge that I needed to come. His amazed and repeated answer was, "Your timing is uncanny." Inside I saw that everything was gone from the house except a chair and an old TV. His partner and her three girls had moved out that morning leaving him destitute and depressed. After spending some time with him I left him in somewhat better spirits. I found out later that he had two more items in the house – a gun and a rope. He was planning to go into the orchard behind the house and commit suicide, but he didn't.

"Aw, he was just plain lucky," objected Jim. "And that's just a made-up story."

"No, Jeb, that was for real. So is the next one."

Personal Crisis

Just before lunch one day I felt a strong sense that I needed to phone a certain lady that my wife and I had counseled recently. Her response on the phone was, "I can't believe you are calling me right now. I've been fasting and praying this morning for an answer from the Lord to a crucial problem in my life and here you have called me. Can you come over right after lunch with your wife?" We did and were able to help her through the issue.

"So you figure you've got a hot line to heaven?" said Jeb.

"I have no special access that isn't available to anyone who earnestly seeks to hear from God," responded Roy. "I'll give you only one more because this is a longer one, but also for real."

The Nail

At 8:30 on a Wednesday morning some years before coming to this town the telephone in my office rang and the voice at the other end asked, "Are you coming?"

"Coming where?" I queried.

"To our Christian School. You promised to provide the devotional today and the students are beginning to gather in the chapel. Are you coming?" continued the inquirer.

"Oh, yes." I replied, "I'll be right there."

I put the receiver down and then it hit me. A five to eight minute drive would get me there but I had not only completely forgotten my commitment, I had prepared no devotional message. What do I do now? Now I am committed to leading a chapel service in less than 10 minutes and I am totally unprepared. I'm ruined! I was serving as a leader in our church telling the volunteers to always be well prepared. Some of them had children in that school. They'll tell their parents about what a flop I was. My Christian service is finished! My life is over!!

Then I remembered a statement I had made to other volunteers. Almost any item around you can be used for an object lesson. I pulled open a drawer of my desk, grabbed an object and headed for the car.

"You've got a problem, Lord," I complained. "No," he said, "You have a problem." "Can we make it our problem?" I pleaded. "Since you put it that way, yes, we can," came the assurance.

On the way out I felt the object in my jacket pocket and began to think. What could this item teach a group of students? In the car my eyes were on the road but my mind was elsewhere. NOT RECOMMENDED!! However, right away ideas began to collect. Verses I'd memorized came into play (I was grateful for a Scripture memorization practice) and an outline formed. Would I be able to remember it? When I got there I looked at the door but really did not want to go in.

Upon arrival the principal was finishing some announcements and then called for me. I was determined to make no apologies or excuses. I would go all out. I might as well go for broke. I held up my hand with the object enclosed in my fist and exclaimed, "Boys and girls, I have in my hand something that will teach you five of the most important lessons you have ever heard. What do think it is?" I could hardly believe I said that. Five most important lessons??!! Would I remember any of them?

After several errant guesses by the students I revealed a nail. This is a brief summary of what I told them.

This nail shows us a number of things about how to live our lives. Pretend you are a carpenter on the job. What kind of nails does he want?

1. **Be Straight**. Carpenters want straight nails. Crooked ones are rejected. Prov. 3:5-6. *Trust in the LORD with all your heart and lean not on your own understanding; in all your ways acknowledge him, and he will make your paths straight.* God wants **us** to be honest and true too.
2. **Be Strong**. A straw may be straight but it isn't strong. A good nail is strong. The Lord is looking for those who will be strong and willing to stand against opposition. Eph. 6:10 *Finally, be strong in the Lord and in his mighty power.*
3. **Be Sharp**. Good nails are sharp. Teachers appreciate sharp students too. They got that way by studying. God also wants followers who are keen in doing their best in all aspects of life, including sincerely searching Scripture to find his will for their lives. It means searching through God's Word for direction in life. 1 Pet. 3:15 *But in your hearts set apart Christ as Lord. Always be prepared to give an answer to everyone who asks you to give the reason for the hope that you have. But do this with gentleness and respect*
4. **Be Solid**. It is great to be straight, strong and sharp but if the nail is pounded into a rotten post none of the above

will help. Ever tried nailing into mud? A solid base is needed. Jesus Christ is our solid foundation. 1 Cor.3:11 *For no one can lay any foundation other than the one already laid, which is Jesus Christ.*

5. Be Struck. None of the above will be of any help at all until the nail is hit on the head. We need to be careful how we apply this idea, but it is true that we learn most lessons when we experience difficulties. We are urged not to despise the discipline of the Lord even though we may feel that we've been hammered. Heb. 12:5 – 6 *"My son, do not make light of the Lord's discipline, and do not lose heart when he rebukes you, because the Lord disciplines those he loves, and he punishes everyone he accepts as a son."*

On the way out one teacher came by and said, "That was very good, just what we needed. You must have prepared a long time."

I didn't quite know what to say but in the few seconds I had before she went to class I think I said, "The Lord does provide."

Later, another person stated that we need a sixth item. God loves to straighten out crooked nails, strengthen weak ones, and sharpen blunt ones. He is in the business of restoring us and meeting our needs. This person was right.

There are more examples but I don't consider myself anything special. However I also do not consider any of these stories I related as just coincidences. The real issue is that it should happen more often, not just occasionally. God does step into our circumstances. I believe he intervened for me in a real way that day."

The men left for their workstations without further remarks. They just had no comment.

Throughout that day Roy earnestly asked for some clear direction from the Lord regarding issues with fellow workers and with David Tyler. What he needed was another divine intervention. That was it! He decided to count on the Lord to engineer a situation where he would be able to respond to the men and to David effectively. Nothing happened that day, or the next, but on the third day at quitting time Roy and David almost bumped in to each other at the exit.

"Mr. Tyler," exclaimed Roy, "good to see you again."

"Hi, Roy," he replied, "how's it going?"

"Pretty good, I'd say, unless you've had more complaints."

"No, I haven't heard a thing so it must be going OK. You've decided to tone it down a few notches I presume."

"I'm not sure I ever turned it up, but I've been thinking about your advice. It doesn't seem right to be one way on Sunday morning and another during the week. One reason for being at a church service is to be spiritually strengthened so that I will put my Christianity into practice all week, not put it on a shelf."

"Church is just a ritual, a personal hobby or a feel-good activity. It's like an escape before you get out into the real world battles. Church is not going to fight any of them for you."

"David, I can't live with myself on that basis. What I believe in or stand for has got to be relevant everywhere all the time or it isn't worth believing in. The Bible tells me to honor the Lord in all I do, words and deeds, all the time, everywhere. He doesn't do that **for** me but he's willing to help me grow spiritually so that I make progress," responded Roy.

"That's your decision. Just don't make trouble here," declared David. "Keep your faith to yourself. I don't want to see you get hurt and I don't want you hurting us either."

There was something about the way David looked and spoke that made Roy uneasy, even suspicious. There's something more to all this than is evident right now, he thought. What could it be?

As if this wasn't unsettling enough Teresa rocked her parents at supper time with some questions they had not expected from her.

"Daddy," she asked, "why does God allow so much pain and suffering to go on in the world?"

Roy and Becky looked at each other as if to see who would tackle this one. Finally Roy spoke up. "That's a good question, Teresa? Lots of people wonder about that one. Did someone talk to you about that or did you just come up with the question yourself?"

"It's been bothering me for weeks, dad. Nobody has talked to me about it."

"Well, Teresa, about all I can say is that people have been given choices and choices have consequences where even innocent people get hurt. How can we expect to make bad choices and have no unpleasant consequences? However, God has provided the way out by sending Jesus as Savior."

"That's another issue, dad. You talk about **the** way out, not **a** way. Other kids are saying that's alright for you but we have our own way. When I talk about Jesus to them they say there are many ways to reach God."

It was becoming clear to Roy that anyone who stands up for Jesus will become a target of some kind, but he hadn't expected it this early in his daughter's life. "Teresa," he explained, "almost every religion or belief system contains some idea of the gap between God and man and how to cross it. Jesus clearly stated that he was the way and no one comes to the Father any other way. This sounds arrogant and exclusive but it is actually loving and kind because none of the other ways will get you there. He's being honest with us. The Holy Spirit is at work all over the world in people's lives and Jesus promised that no one who comes to him will be turned away. He accepts them all so he is very inclusive, not exclusive."

"When I say things like that to them they say that I'm just parroting the Bible. What proof have I got that it is true. Maybe it's just another collection of religious writings."

This really set Roy back on his heels because he had not thought that Teresa would ever say things like that. She had been his joy to talk to rather deeply about many issues of faith and he had not expected doubts to come into it. Becky stepped in and said, "Teresa, you've been a brave girl to even talk about such things to others. You are to be congratulated and those questions are fair game. As to the reliability of the Bible I keep reminding myself of the answer your dad has given to others a number of times. Any book that claims to be from God would have to ring true to life, come true in its predictions 100% of the time and be able to transform lives, make them true. There is only one book that has consistently been able to do that for centuries. It is the Bible."

"OK mom and dad. That does help."

"In the end," ventured Roy, "we either count on it to be true by faith or count on it not to be true, also by faith. We have a choice."

The meal ended on a somewhat somber note but the challenges to Roy's faith did not stop there. The next sentence in Denver's letter captured the issue.

"We could all tell the days when you had some gut-wrenching encounters with some guy at work. You'd be home but not really there. You'd be preoccupied with whatever controversy was the theme for the day."

"Hey, Roy," called Jeb at the beginning of lunch break a few days later. "Is your hot-line to heaven sizzling today?" Guffaws of laughter followed from Jim and Jeb. (Vulgarities omitted from the conversation) "Yeah," scoffed Jim. "Really sizzling as God fries a few more people in hell. Did he tell you he's got a reservation there for Jeb and me? See if you can get an air conditioner put in for us." More laughter.

Roy was reluctant to respond. Would it simply add fuel to the 'fire'!!? Yet to say nothing would be to admit defeat.

"You've hit upon a valid concern, guys. Hell is a tough concept to handle. It is described as a lake of fire but also as the blackness of darkness. For this reason I don't think it could be a literal fire designed to torture. The bottom line is about a final separation from God. Unbelievers are telling God to stay out of their lives and in the end they get what they asked for."

"Oh, I see," mocked Jeb. "He sends you into torment but he's still a God of love. What a bunch of baloney."

"God doesn't send anyone to hell. Anyone who ends up there has gone there by choice."

"That's a bunch of hogwash!" exploded Jim. (Vulgarities omitted)

"Give me a chance to explain it this way, guys," offered Roy. "Suppose the two of you had started a manufacturing plant like this from scratch and built it up to the place where it was a huge business. I was one of your employees but I refused to do things the way you wanted them. I did what pleased me, used whatever I wanted for my own benefit, ignored instructions and defied your authority. What would you do?"

"You'd be outa there so fast you wouldn't know what hit you," growled Jim.

"You'd be right to do that, but suppose instead you came to me and made an offer. Suppose you told me that you really cared about me and would pay for all the damages, continue to provide for me and give me a privileged position in spite of what I had done. You'd forgive all that had happened if I were willing to acknowledge my wrongs and accept your authority. What if I rejected that offer?" asked Roy.

"That deal would never happen and if you treated us like that you'd be out on the garbage dump!" shouted Jim.

"That is how we react as people, but it isn't God's way. This planet, the air we breathe, the water we drink, the food that is grown, our bodies, and a vast number of other things we depend on for life are made by God for us. They are like gifts. He loves us. How are we treating him in response? Do we use it all, take it for granted and ignore everything he asks of us? Do we respond when he makes the ultimate offer of personally paying for every wrong we've done by dying for us on the cross in the Person of his Son? He's saying that if you insist on going to hell you'll have to go over my dead body. What do you mean that he sends people there? Anyone who goes there does so because they chose it," insisted Roy.

"Ah, that's a bunch of crap," blared Jeb, as he and Jim stomped out of there. (Vulgarities omitted)

Sam had been quiet, taking it all in, but it was clear that he was not about to restrain himself anymore. As soon as he began some sort of a blanket of respect came over the group that was left.

"Roy," began Sam, his voice rising in intensity as he progressed. "I don't see how you can accept a concept like hell and still claim that you have a loving God. If he's perfect and only makes perfect things how come his prize specimen went so wrong? Maybe he should take the blame? What a cruel thing to allow someone to go to hell forever when they didn't even ask to be born into the world, especially not with a nature inclined toward doing wrong, as your Bible says. I find the idea so repulsive it makes me angry to think of it."

"I don't have all the answers, Sam. I guess we'll just have to ask God himself when we meet him, which could be soon. One thing I do know, Genesis 18:25 declares *'Shall not the Judge of all the earth do right?'* God is a God of love and compassion but he is also a God of holiness and justice. Sam, I appreciate your concern but I have no other answer."

"That is not good enough for me," responded Sam. "I reject that idea and with it the whole concept of being Christian. There are better ways."

"You said it, Sam!" came the approval of most of the crew. "Those explanations stink!"

Lunch was over and they all headed back to work. Roy was less than encouraged.

Denver was right on in the next sentence of his letter. "Your impact on the men at work became a major focus in your life. I wish we could have found a meaning for life for me too."

A twinge of guilt made Roy hurt deep inside as he realized that he had been able to help some fellow workers but not really solve a major issue for his son.

Chapter 9

What's all this about Salvation?

On the next evening together, after a time of getting more acquainted with Roy's family, Tom and Harry came right out with a major concern.

"We've been thinking about that discussion on hell, Roy. It really bothers us. When the Bible talks about being saved I guess it means saved from hell, right?" asked Harry.

"That's definitely a major part of it."

"You mean it's more than that? What is this salvation idea all about anyway?" asked Tom. "I've heard all kinds of talk about being born again but most of those Christians don't seem to be any better than I am. Others seem to set up a bunch of rules to obey that will get you into heaven. I just figure that if I treat people right and do the best I can I'll be OK. Isn't that good enough?"

"The idea of salvation is a critical subject, guys. It's all about dealing with sin, namely who's going to pay? Most people don't want to talk about sin but it is problem number one in life."

"But lots of us are doing the best we can. Isn't that good enough for God? He's supposed to be a God of love, not Somebody with a club looking for guys he can hammer," responded Tom.

"God is love," agreed Roy, "but he is also holy and just. He wanted to find a way to reach out to people in love and still be just and holy. Being a just and holy God means that every sin will be dealt with. He cannot ignore even one sin and still be fully just. He has found the solution for this problem."

"He has?" exclaimed Harry. "How did he do it?"

Roy answered, "First he did not lower his standards. Sin had to be fully paid for and the wages of sin is death we are told in Rom. 6:23. Somebody had to die. So that was the sentence imposed. Then he turned around and offered to pay the price himself in the Person of his Son, Jesus. He literally takes the blame for our wrongs. That's why Jesus was crucified. He will take our place and pay the bill if we admit we need it and ask him to. How could we object to, or reject, that kind of an offer? Not only does he take our sin upon himself, but in exchange he credits us with his righteousness. It's like having a rich man offer to trade his bank account for a beggar's debts. Now that is some deal!"

"Never thought of it that way," pondered Tom.

"Listen," objected Harry. "If God is just he also needs to consider the good deeds. What if they balance out and cancel the bad ones? Isn't that fair?"

"If they actually did balance out we'd have something to talk about but God has already given us the answer to that one. *All have sinned and fall short Rom. 3:23*. In another place God says, '*He saved us, not because of righteous things we had done but because of His mercy' Titus 3:5*. In fact, Harry, there's a verse in Isaiah that puts it really bluntly. It says that even our most righteous acts are like filthy rags in God's sight when it comes to doing away with sin. Harry, God says there is only one way. Let Jesus handle it for you. We are incapable of paying the bill."

"But that's such a narrow way of looking at it. What makes Christians think they are the only ones that are right. That's awfully arrogant!" objected Tom.

"It's not our idea, Tom," replied Roy. "As the One who made and owns it all, God sets the rules, not us. How can we argue with him?"

"It's asking an awful lot to accept that," objected Harry. "I'd have to think hard on that one."

"Me too," muttered Tom.

After some more questions and some light chatter about other things as they finished off the goodies Becky provided, the two left for home with the commitment to come back next week.

When they returned a week later Harry came prepared. "What if I did ask Jesus to handle the sin problem for me and the next day sin again. Now I'm short again so what was the use?"

"Look, you guys. Here's the full deal about salvation that will answer that question, "responded Roy. "This offer first of all provides peace with God by having sin paid for and its penalty out of the way. This is a continuing arrangement because 1 John 2:1 – 2 tells us *'My dear children, I write this to you so that you will not sin. But if anybody does sin, we have one who speaks to the Father in our defense – Jesus Christ, the Righteous One.'* Jesus is an ongoing attorney for the defense. So that difficulty is looked after."

"That's like getting carte blanche to sin," remarked Tom. "If Jesus is going to pay for every sin I commit even after I become a Christian I can do whatever I feel like. That's crazy!"

"You're right, Tom," agreed Harry. "This is getting ridiculous."

"Guys, there's more to the story. A person who has come to Jesus for salvation from sin is coming because he or she has concluded that sin is a big problem, it's a bummer, it wrecks lives. Why would that person then want to go out and sin at will? Furthermore, since Jesus paid for sin with his own life would the person who accepts that gift not want to do everything he or she could to please him? That is the second aspect of salvation. It amounts to learning how to have victory over the power of sin in our lives after we become Christians. It also includes repentance as an essential ingredient. Repentance means that the person has decided to turn from sin and pursue righteousness, not to earn salvation but because he/she already has it. The important thing to settle first is the question of how to have peace with God, or freedom from the penalty of sin."

"I don't think I've been at war with Him so why do we need a peace agreement?" countered Harry.

"God wanted things to go a certain way and we tend to go a different way, a very different way. This does make us his enemies. He says as much in Romans 5:10. Sin makes us at odds with God and God refuses to allow even one sin in heaven. We have to get rid of sin somehow," explained Roy.

"Are we really that bad?" asked Tom. "Many of us try to live good lives. Isn't that enough?"

"We simply have an inadequate picture of sin," answered Roy. "Simply put it's like Romans 3:23 says, *All have sinned and fall short of the glory of God.*"

Roy explained the steps to peace with God. Harry was ready to respond but Tom wasn't so sure. The question arose again about trying to live the Christian life afterwards. What if we sin again?

"Let me try to explain again," offered Roy. "There is much confusion and difference of opinion about the experience of salvation. So much of the Bible concentrates on God's displeasure with evil and his delight in righteousness that it is easy to see why some would conclude that salvation is for those who have lived a good enough life. How do we reconcile the clear moral standards of God with his offer of grace - salvation as a gift to anyone? I believe the following passage will clarify that when we realize that in God's view, salvation comes in three aspects.

Let's read 1 Peter 1:3-9. From these verses we may well wonder if salvation is a past event, a present experience or a future fulfillment. It speaks of salvation as a past event (vs.3), a present challenge (vs.7-9) and a future prospect (vs. 5). Therefore the only answer is that it is all three. There are three aspects to salvation in God's plan: past, present and future."

Tom asked, "Are you saying that it isn't a one-time emotional event like you see at a Billy Graham crusade?"

"It may well begin that way," replied Roy, "and that is an important happening because that is one place where some people do become Christians but it doesn't stop there. Conversion is where the debt of sin is paid off, but people who become Christians don't completely stop doing things wrong. We sin too. What we need now is the power to reduce that influence in our lives. It isn't until life is over that we are completely removed from sin being present in our lives."

"But if we sin again after becoming a Christian what was the point? We're no better off," argued Harry.

"Yes, we are better off, much better off because Jesus has taken on paying for that problem," replied Roy. "It's like being born into a family. Your son will always be part of your family even if he misbehaves. The goal is to have him grow out of those difficulties. That's why you teach and even discipline him."

"You mean God is like a father," asked Tom.

"Yup," assured Roy. "He starts by giving us a gift according to Eph. 2:8-9. There salvation is called a gift from God. When it comes to living like a Christian after that, Hebrews 12 shows it as a discipline. When life is over it is time for the awards assembly. We can read about that in 2 Cor. 5:10 and 1 Cor. 3:11 - 15. That's when we are completely out of the reach of sin."

"It's beginning to sound like a good plan," mused Harry.

"I see it this way," responded Roy. "As a gift salvation is a **done deal** when the penalty of sin is paid. While we are living as Christians on earth, life can be a **tough deal** at times but in the end when the Lord takes us home it will be a **new deal**. Let me give you a chart that lists the comparisons and refers you to verses in the Bible where the ideas come from. That way you can study up on it for yourself."

"OK," agreed Tom. "That sounds fair."

"Alright, I'll get some copies from my files right now," said Roy.

When Roy returned he gave them each a copy with this comment.

"If you have already decided to trust Christ for salvation you are in the middle column until he takes you home to himself. Does that make sense, guys?" asked Roy.

"It's beginning to," responded Tom. "I've got to take that chart home and think about it some more."

"OK," replied Roy. "That's a good move. Suppose we get you to share what you came up with when we get together next week."

"Deal," agreed Harry. "See you then." (See Appendix 1 for a copy of the chart.)

Chapter 10

Suspicions Mount

"Hey, Roy," called the foreman, Gary, a few days later as Roy came to work. "I need to switch you over to another job for a bit. Usually Jeb does this kind of work but he's away today. We've got an RV here that has been labeled deficient in a major way and is destined for referral to a more capable repair shop. But I need confirmation that this is really true about the RV. Here's the deficiency analysis. Check it out for me, OK? Kirk is expecting to pick it up in the morning as a job for him if it is needed."

"Sure," promised Roy. "This looks like something I can handle so I'll get at it right away."

It took Roy a very short while to spot what the problem was. Several reconnections and adjustments later the unit was in perfect working order. The wrong connections were in the oddest places, hidden away and hard to spot for someone not familiar with the way it was supposed to be. Faulty adjustments increased the problem so that it was easy to see why the unit would not perform. But it completely baffled Roy how something like that could have happened. He filed the work order, complete with explanations and declared the unit in very good shape. He told Gary what he had found and went back to his regular work.

Early next morning Roy spotted Kirk just as he was hauling the very same unit away. He asked Gary about it and was told that Jeb had come in and told him that the unit was still not functioning as it should and so they hauled it away. Something smelled rotten here. Roy could not shake the feeling that something suspicious was going on. He was sure the unit was in perfect working order when he finished with it. There would not have even been sufficient time for Jeb to do a thorough check on it before it was hauled away. This was not right!

Roy decided to confide in Harry who had worked here a long time.

"Harry, I am puzzled and suspicious about something. Yesterday Gary asked me to check out an RV destined for referral to Kirk's shop and I did check it out. I found the problem which consisted of several most unusual wrong connections and adjustments. When I did the reconnections and proper adjustments everything worked smoothly. Yet this morning I saw Kirk hauling it away as a job for his shop. Jeb had claimed it was still malfunctioning. He had barely been at work a few minutes before Kirk came for it. What's going on?" wondered Roy.

"I've been suspicious for months about this arrangement between Jeb, Kirk and David, the Sales Manager. For the last year or so there have been an unusually large number of units referred to Jeb for confirmation and hauled away by Kirk. Each one of them is a referral by David for inspection by Jeb and pickup by Kirk. What you have just told me makes it smell really bad."

"What do we do? Should we just turn a blind eye and not get involved?"

"That would be the easy way out. If we are going to jump in we'd better have all our ducks in order. We need evidence, solid evidence or else stay out of it."

"That means we keep our eyes open for conclusive evidence without tipping our hand," ventured Roy.

"Got it! And we're on track for some right now."

Harry and Roy went their separate ways, both wondering what this would develop into. Over the next few weeks things took on a calmer look at work, Harry and Tom responded to the gospel and were growing significantly and Roy continued to be very involved in the church. It seemed to him that all was well, but was it?

Denver's letter continued. "For you it was great because some important things were coming to a head at work. I know that you wanted to earnestly serve the Lord and I respect that but for me life was getting to mean less and less." The words hit him like a brick but some defensive thoughts also crossed his mind. "Denver, it was you who got involved in other things and drifted away. It was not just me being drawn to other things. I had tried hard for two years!" He could see how the trend had developed as he recalled a surprising turn of events at work.

Chapter 11

Gary Opens Up

A few days later as Roy was packing away some tools after all the others had already cleared out, the foreman, Gary, approached him hesitatingly.

"Something wrong?" asked Roy, wondering if there would be another complaint.

"No, Roy. You've been doing a great job. In fact I've noticed a positive influence from you on the men. I appreciate that. Mind if I ask you about something?" inquired Gary.

"Not at all," replied Roy, "go ahead."

"This is kind of tough for me to talk about but I'm having troubles at home. I just don't seem to know how to relate to my kids effectively. I've watched you relate to the men and to your kids when they come around after work. Maybe you could give me some pointers."

Inside Roy winced a bit at the compliment but he did not let it show.

"Glad to," replied Roy. "But it would take some time. We could both call home and let our wives know that we'd be about half an hour late."

"My wife wouldn't care," replied Gary.

"That could be a big part of the problem, Gary. The best thing you can do for your kids is to love your wife and treat her with respect and consideration. Perhaps it would be a pleasant surprise for her if you called to explain."

"Well, OK," shrugged Gary reluctantly. "Let's go to my office and call, then talk."

When the calls were made and the arrangements in place Roy started his response.

"Gary, let's get into this by using an angle you are familiar with, namely, your fellow workers here. OK?"

"Sure," agreed Gary.

"What do you expect the men to have or be able to do when they show up for work?"

"They need some know-how," responded Gary.

"Right," agreed Roy. "Anything else?"

"Attitude helps a lot. If they don't care how they do it, knowing how doesn't mean much," offered Gary. "Without the right attitude you'll likely do a poor job."

"True, you've hit on two of the most important things," said Roy. "Is there anything else that could prevent a guy from doing the job right even if he knew how and wanted to do it right?"

"Can't see what that would be unless they just didn't have the knack for the job," mused Gary.

"It would take something like that or maybe injury, sickness or some serious stress or depression to sidetrack a good man," ventured Roy, "but that could happen. Right?"

"Guess so, but what has that got to do with my family?" argued Gary.

"Lots, Gary. We as parents want our kids to do what's right just like men on a job. That's good, but they aren't going to measure up to that all the time because one or more of those three things is deficient. They are either lacking in knowledge, don't have the right attitude or are short on ability. We need to learn how to deal with where they are at without destroying our relationship. Look at it this way. For anyone in your family to do the right thing he/she needs to have developed enough of the same three aspects we just mentioned. They are the same ones that the guys need here in the plant to do a job right. They need the right knowledge or facts, the right attitude or value system and the ability to do it."

"Yup, I guess that's it," agreed Gary.

"So, if you are having trouble with your kids it may be because one or more of the three are not in good shape. If it is lack of knowledge you need to find a way to explain. If it is a bad attitude you need to figure out what would motivate them. If the ability to do what you want is not there you need to find out what it would take to develop that ability or how to direct them toward something they can do. Makes sense?"

"Ya, it does but I'm afraid the diagnosis is going to be the easy part. Finding the remedy would be the tough part."

"Right, Gary. That's true for all of us. Often if the attitude is right the rest will fall into place. This means that building a relationship with each of your kids is the key."

"But how can I relate to them or motivate them if they don't want to have anything to do with me?"

"That's a tough one. You have to spot an interest or potential they have and encourage them in it, show that you care and want them to succeed. Recognize even tiny progress and give them praise."

"There's no easy answer, is there?" moaned Gary.

"Definitely not, "responded Roy, as he winced inside himself about not measuring up to his own advice. "It's not easy for me either. Tell you what. You need a chance to read and think about what we've discussed. I'll bring a chart on paper that summarizes these things and we could go over it together tomorrow so that it would be clearer to you what your options are. Then you have to decide what to do. OK?"

Faith Under Fire

"Alright," agreed Gary. "See you tomorrow after work. And I'll tell my wife."

The next day Roy gave Gary a copy of the chart and explanations accompanying it. (Turn to Appendix 2 if you want to see it.) They worked through it together.

"OK, Roy," replied Gary. "I'll give it a whirl. Thanks for the help."

"Let's get together again real soon to see how you are doing. Don't expect to solve everything overnight, and don't get too discouraged if you blow it."

"OK, Roy," smiled Gary. He felt like he at least had a bit of a handle on things now. Roy felt a tinge of guilt creeping in as he thought about times when he hadn't given his own family the priority he should have. And here he was urging Gary to do it. There was again this nagging thought in the back of his mind that something wasn't quite right at home. Isn't there some way in which a positive witness at work, a ministry in the church and a quality relationship at home could all be maintained?

Roy was still pondering this question on Thursday after getting home from work when he saw Teresa coming home from band practice at school. She was literally bouncing up the driveway, obviously in high spirits. "Mom, dad," she called as she came through the door. "Guess what!"

"You must be excited about something," answered Becky. "Did you ace your Chem test?"

"Naw, nothing as boring as that. I've been invited to a party!" she beamed.

"What kind of a party is this, Teresa?" asked Roy cautiously.

"It's at the home of one of the senior high girls but they are including me even though I'm only in Grade 9. Isn't that neat!"

An orange flag went up in the back of Becky's mind. "Which girl is this and is it for girls only?" she asked.

"Oh, mom. Right away you get suspicious. It's just an innocent fun time. You can trust us."

"Did they tell you what they'd be doing?" queried Roy.

"It's just a party, dad. We're just having fun. What's wrong with that? You're making it sound like there is trouble already. Can't you just trust us?"

"If I knew the home and knew what was going on I could answer that question. I don't know either the family or the plan so how can I blindly trust? There have been some very disastrous results from parties like that. Who is this girl that's inviting you?"

"It's Tammy Provost. I think you know her dad because he works at the same place you do."

"Jim Provost! Yes, I do know him." For Roy this wasn't just an orange flag, it was bright red. Jim was the friend of Jeb at work. The two of them were against all he stood for and had abusively expressed their opposition to his Christianity.

"Teresa, when is this supposed to happen?" asked Becky.

"Tomorrow night. We get to sleep over and I'd be back some time on Saturday."

"Teresa," continued Roy, "your mom and I will talk about it and get back to you later tonight."

"What's there to talk about? I'm 15 already. Don't I get to choose some things for myself?"

"Some things, yes. This item, no," declared Roy.

Teresa stomped off to her room.

Roy filled Becky in on what he already knew about Jim, the father of Tammy. They decided that a call to the home would be in order. When Roy called and asked for Jim it was Tammy who said he was not available. When asked when he could be reached she said it would be Monday because her mom and dad were out of town for the weekend.

The scene was a stormy one when Roy and Becky confronted Teresa with the situation. This setup at the Provost home did not look good or healthy. Teresa would not be going. It hurt the parents that their daughter just didn't see the danger in this but they stuck to their decision.

By Monday the news was all over town. A riot had broken out at an unsupervised teen-aged all night party that had been crashed by some uninvited guys. Liquor, drugs and who knows what else were evident when the police were called by the neighbors during the night. Teresa was subdued and thanked her parents for standing firm. Roy and Becky were encouraged by Teresa's reaction.

But Denver's letter kept hitting him hard. "It really rocked me when you got into marriage counseling while mom was getting worse and your attention less." Roy had to sit down as the impact of this set in. He could see it all now. He had so much wanted to do things right at work and in the community while taking for granted that things were going right at home.

Chapter 12

Seven Musts of Marriage

"Hey, Gary," said Roy when no one else was around, "how's it been going at home since we last talked?"

"Well, I've made a little progress, Roy," ventured Gary, "but perhaps the only real progress is that now I know where I'm using the wrong approach. Making sure I do the right thing is tough when the emotions boil over. I just don't stop and think long enough to get it right."

"Gary, you have made progress if you are recognizing what's wrong. Don't give up. Did you know that there is Someone very interested in giving you the power to deal with that?"

"I suppose you'll want to bring God into this."

"I couldn't get to first base without him there for me, Gary, but that is something you have to decide for yourself."

"I've been thinking about it. Tell me, does this work in the marriage relationship too?"

"Yes, some of it applies. There is a more specific set of ideas that might be helpful to you if you are interested but I am not a professional marriage counselor."

"I'd still like us to get together about it. We are having big problems in our marriage and I think you could help."

"I'd have to be honest with you that this set up is all drawn from the Bible. You see, a breakdown in marriage relationships is one of the chief means the devil uses to attack society, break up families and discredit Christians too. Does that change your idea about hearing what the plan is?"

"Let me think about that, Roy. If I decide to go ahead with it I'll get back to you and we can set up a time."

"OK, Gary. Glad to help you if you want it."

A few days later Gary said that he would listen to what Roy had to say but would make no promises about applying it or even accepting what the plan contained. Roy understood and agreed. They set up a time for an evening in the coming week.

After a few minutes of informal chatting in Roy and Becky's home a week later, Roy explained to Gary that this was his own perception of what the Bible's standard was for marriage. Those who applied what it taught would have a more solid marriage relationship. Here is a brief summary of the **Seven Musts of Marriage** as Roy explained them to Gary.

Provider - Both must contribute a fair share of ability and energy to tasks that make the practical side of marriage work. They need to agree on what jobs each will do. Scripture makes it clear that if we do not provide for our own family we are worse than an infidel. (1 Tim.5:8).

Enthusasm for life - This definitely implies that a negative attitude to life is not suitable for marriage. We each need to bring some excitement into the relationship! The Lord came to give life and to give it abundantly. (Jn. 10:10)

Respect - The woman is to respect her husband and the husband needs to respect his wife. Without that kind of an attitude the relationship will not work. (Eph. 5:33)

Faithful morally - Many marriage breakups are caused by marital unfaithfulness. We are to be true to one partner. (Matthew 5:28, 1 Cor. 6:18)

Endearment and encouragement – It is imperative for the man to love his wife. Clearly the wife must also love her husband. (Eph.5:25)

Christian commitment - For marriage to work a Christian needs to marry another Christian. When both have a personal commitment to follow the Lord much potential difficulty is weeded out. We know that there are couples that have made their marriage work without any indication of a Christian commitment, by having the same value system. (2 Cor.6:14) But in the end it's their relationship to God that is the issue.

Thrift - Money plays a large role in marriage difficulties. Sensible money management principles are a must in marriage. (1 Tim. 6:10; Prov. 31:10 - 25)

    So there you have it, Gary. Pretty big load to dump on you all at once, eh!"
    "You said it, Roy!"
    "What do you notice about the first letter of each of the seven categories?"
    "What do you mean?"
    "If you take the first letter of each of the seven titles what word does it spell?"
    "P-E-R-F-E-C-T. It spells perfect. No wonder it's out of reach."

"Exactly," assured Roy. "The problem is that there are no perfect marriages, certainly not ours. Couples are sort of half dreaming and half hoping that they will have a perfect marriage when they have their wedding but it is unrealistic. No couple is 100% on all seven counts. However, we can get a good part of the way in each one."

"This is for Christians only," declared Gary. "Wouldn't help me."

"I suppose people could delete the Scripture verses and change **Christian Commitment** to **Commitment to a Common Set of Values.** Then it wouldn't look so religious even though the principles come from the Bible. The big drawback would be that the strength God can give to live up to these would be lacking. I have faith that God can make the difference."

"I dunno, Roy," moaned Gary. "It's all so overwhelming. I sometimes just feel like giving up and throwing in the towel. I don't know what to do, or maybe I know what to do but don't want to do it."

"About all I can do now, Gary, is pray for you and I will be doing that."

"Thanks, Roy. I've really got to do some thinking so I'll take this copy with me if you don't mind."

"You are welcome to it. Let's meet again soon but it should be as couples in order for it to help."

"Ya, OK. All this stuff is making a little difference so don't think I don't appreciate what you are saying. It's just so overwhelming." With that Gary said "Good night" and went home.

Conviction descended on Roy as he watched Gary leave. "What am I doing," he asked himself? "Here I am telling Gary how to relate to his children and his wife and I'm not doing those things well myself. I've just got to make changes! I've got to make tonight and future days meaningful for all of them."

Neither Denver nor Teresa were home for supper or for the evening. They both had "other" things going. It did give Roy an opportunity to interact with Becky privately.

"They are nearly grown-up, Roy," replied Becky. "Denver has graduated and is working at a job. Teresa is in her final year in Senior High School. We can't expect them to be at home with us all the time."

"No, you're right, but I was kind of hoping they would be tonight. It would also be different if I knew that they were involved in wholesome, Christ-honoring things but I have the impression they are drifting away from the Lord. Do you see it that way?"

"Yes, it's true. They don't have the interest in spiritual things that they used to have. They're still good kids and we have lots to be thankful for, but I am also concerned."

"How are you doing in terms of your health, Becky?"

"Probably as expected. I'm not getting younger and it is not improving so I guess it is slowly taking its toll. Otherwise I'm OK."

"I haven't been there for you recently like I should, Becky, but I just don't know what I can do to help. I wish I could fix it for good. We've prayed for healing and sought the Lord for answers but there seem to be none. I think it's affecting Denver's faith because he really counts on you."

"We've talked about it many times and he knows what will happen unless the Lord chooses to intervene. I'm trying to prepare him for it. Are you ready for it when it comes?"

"No, I'm not and I doubt if I ever will be. I just don't want to even think about it."

At this point they heard Denver coming into the driveway.

"Hi, son. How was your day?" asked Roy.

"Not too bad, dad," answered Denver, "how about you?"

"Good, yes, it was a good day."

"Feelin' OK today, mom?"

"As good as I can expect, Denver."

"That tells me it is not good. Are you having constant pain?"

"It's there most of the time but I am used to it."

Denver's tone changed. "It's not fair," he exclaimed. "Why is God allowing this? Why don't our prayers get answered? Didn't he promise to hear us when we ask?"

"Sometimes his answer is No, Denver," replied Becky.

"Then my answer is No too," stormed Denver. "Why should I serve a God like that?"

"He has given us a huge number of good things, Denver," responded Roy. "We have to accept the things we don't like too. I am also upset that mom hasn't been healed. I hate seeing it go this way but feeling resentment that way won't help."

"Denver, our spiritual health is more important than our physical health. I will be completely healed when I get that glorious new body Philippians 3:21 talks about," offered Becky.

"That won't do anything for me now," objected Denver. "I think I'd better go to my room and go to bed. I'm no help here. I also have an early start at work tomorrow so I'll just say good night."

"Have a good sleep, son," replied Roy.

Both Roy and Becky sat up for a long time, hardly speaking and mostly just reflecting on the conversation just finished. It was late when Teresa walked in, past her curfew for school nights.

"Hi, mom and dad. You still up? You look a bit down in the mouth. Is that because I'm late again? I am nearly 18 already and next year I expect to be on my own at university. You've got to trust me more," stated Teresa.

"Teresa, we've just had a chat with Denver and he is upset because your mom's health hasn't improved. He's afraid of losing her. That is what made us look depressed," explained Roy.

"Oh, sorry, I didn't know that. Is it really bad, mom? I don't mean to make things worse for you."

"Not that bad, Teresa. But we have to be honest with you both. Added to that concern is a more important one. We sense that you are both losing interest in spiritual things and we are worried about where that will lead to," added Becky.

"Don't worry about us, mom and dad," exclaimed Teresa in an exasperated voice, "we'll be just fine. You've got to let us make our own decisions."

"Teresa, we are concerned because we care, not because we want to control," explained Roy.

"But you still want us to do things they way you did them. Anyway, I've got to get to bed. See you all in the morning. And mom, I really do hope that you get better. It hurts to see you like this."

The three of them all headed for bed, but Roy and Becky didn't sleep for quite a while. Roy told her about his chats with Gary and his feelings of guilt about what was happening at home. They prayed together and finally fell asleep.

The next lines in the letter cut like a knife. "You talked to us about how you faced the conflict that was brewing at work. It involved making good decisions. I couldn't help but wonder if the right decision was being made about mom." Roy could picture that episode too. Here he'd been telling others about perfect marriages and then told them how to make good decisions. It tormented Roy to think that Denver saw this as a bit of hypocrisy. He remembered how Jeb had also used the decision-making item against him.

Chapter 13

Decisions! Decisions!

At lunch the group complained about Gary's latest decision. "He just jumps to conclusions by pulling something out of the air," complained Jeb. "Does he think that we know nothing?"

"Yeah," added Tom. "We've got some brains in this group too. Take Roy there as an example. He's always got an organized answer for everything."

"Whether we like it or not, right?" laughed Sam. "Give us another one of your gems on this one, Roy."

"Look, you guys. Making decisions is a tough challenge. Right now Gary is under a lot of stress so let's go easy on him. I don't know enough about this case to come up with an answer so I am in no position to criticize Gary," responded Roy.

"Does he know enough about our situation to make a decision?" asked another worker.

"Sounds to me like we need to be talking about process before we can say anything about how right or wrong a decision is," ventured Roy.

"I don't get it," replied Jim.

"Well, it's like this. You've got to investigate before you castigate or legislate."

There was a silent pause before Sam asked, "Is that all you've got to say?"

"No, there are a number of different means we commonly use to reach a conclusion or make a decision. If you ask me to explain them it will sound like I'm putting you back into a high school class. Is that what you want?"

"No school class for me!" shouted Jim angrily. "What's this about several different ways of doing it? We've just got to take our stand and sock it to him!" (Vulgarities omitted)

"We've got to do it the right way," answered Roy.

"Why not listen to these magic ways he's found," joked Jeb, "Then we can pull his ideas apart, right?"

"Not a chance," stormed Jim and stalked off with most of the men following. A handful stayed and goaded Roy into explaining himself. (If you want to read what that discussion was, turn to Appendix 5.)

Roy noticed Jeb taking notes during the explanation and was encouraged by that. The rest nodded and Sam confirmed his impression that this is another ideal formula that looks good on paper but doesn't necessarily work in real day to day life.

A few days later Roy was called into Gary's office. The look on Gary's face and the body language did not bode well for the discussion.

"I hear you've been telling the guys that I should do more investigation before I make decisions. I should be explaining and encouraging the guys more," blurted Gary, the foreman. "I consider that to be an undermining move."

"Gary, I did no such thing," responded Roy. "Where did you get that idea?"

"One of the guys wrote down what you said word for word. You stated things like *'decisions should not be made without investigation'* and *'no excuse for hasty decisions'* and *'most comments should explain or encourage'*. That sounds clear enough to me as starting trouble. Here I was coming to you for advice and this is what you do to me!"

"The fellows were asking me for my take on how people reach decisions and I described 6 different ways that I knew of. Investigation just happens to be one of them and was not directed as a complaint against anyone," argued Roy. "Then they asked me what I thought about how to communicate a decision. These ideas apply to all situations in general. I wasn't talking about you."

"You're just trying to cover up, Roy. The guys know it was directed at me," complained Gary. "There's been trouble here ever since all those arguments you've been having with the guys at coffee break and lunch time. It just has to stop."

"We've been having discussions, not arguments. The only ones who get angry or upset are Jeb and Jim. Say, is Jeb the one who claimed I am starting trouble and undermining you?"

"I'm not revealing sources," stated Gary. "It's confidential."

"Did your source also report my statement that *"We don't know all that Gary was facing in this situation. We'd better find out more before we object.'* I was supporting you, not fighting you."

"I don't buy that," declared Gary. "You're being moved to another line in the plant as of tomorrow morning. I've just had enough. Discussion ended! You may leave!"

Roy left the plant in a dejected state of mind. He had thought things were going so well. The very person he thought he had built a trusting relationship with had turned against him. Now he was being falsely accused, given no recourse and forced to leave the place that had begun to produce results. At home his family noticed the change in his demeanor from the day before. For Denver and Teresa it just confirmed their desire to stay away from such encounters. Becky was sympathetic and supportive, assuring him that God had not abandoned him and things would work out for the better in some way. It cheered him up somewhat. He looked at Becky appreciatively, and then his demeanor expressed some alarm. "Becky," he declared. "Something is the matter. You don't look well."

"I've been feeling rough lately," she admitted.

"You didn't tell me you were having a hard time," implored Roy. "Why didn't I see it sooner?"

"You were busy and preoccupied with a lot of other concerns, Roy," declared Becky. "I didn't want to interfere with that."

"You mean I was so taken up with what was happening at church, at work, in my class and in the small group that I didn't see what was happening to you?"

"I guess so, Roy. But don't beat yourself up about it. The doctors say they can't help me so what could you do?"

"I at least needed to be there for you. Becky, I've let things slip. I am sorry for not seeing this, so very sorry. Will you forgive me?"

"Why certainly, Roy. You've been a pillar for me for years."

Becky had been a major source of encouragement for him, but he could also see that her physical strength and emotional stamina had waned. He worried about how she was going to cope with her deteriorating condition. So many things were piling up on him at a time when he needed to be strong for Becky.

Back at the plant the next day Roy reported to his new place of work. The guys there seemed wary of him, as though they had been forewarned. It was not a pleasant feeling. Did he dare to raise any questions for discussion at all? It was so unfair. He decided to keep to himself as much as possible. He was in no mood to talk.

Adding to the troubles were the repeated complaints about the work place from his son, Denver. He talked about quitting and moving away. It seemed that the wrong set of guys were willing to associate with him while the more "acceptable" ones were ignoring him. The Youth Pastor at church tried to help and the young adults group was a better scene but it didn't carry over into life at work. Teresa was losing interest in spiritual things too since she was gaining in popularity and recognition at the school. All this brought on a low period in Roy's life to the point where he withdrew from some responsibilities at the church, postponed his meetings with Harry and Tom and began to seek solitude at work. Life was losing the luster it had a few weeks ago. But he kept his promise to be there more often for Becky.

Tom and Harry noted Roy's dejected state. They decided to confront him and bring him around, using his own teaching "against" him. They found him outside the plant after work one day.

"Roy," chided Harry, "you aren't doing so well lately. I don't blame you. You've been handed a raw deal. But we've been depending on you to be there for us."

Roy chafed a bit under the rebuke but he knew they meant well.

"You're right, Harry, but I just can't cope. Maybe this will show you that in the end you have to count on the Lord for strength, not on me."

"Roy, that is true and right now we need to be there for you. What can we do to help?" asked Tom.

"Stay with me. Don't give up on me. On top of what is happening at work Becky is dying, Denver is having trouble at work and Teresa is drifting away from the Lord. I need your support," admitted Roy.

"That is rough. We didn't know it was all that bad. We'll be there for you, Roy," promised Harry. "We both made a commitment to trust the Lord for our salvation and for strength to live right. Now is the time to prove it."

The time spent with the two men did make a difference. Roy was encouraged by their care for him. But Roy was yet to experience the full blast of despair. Becky's condition worsened. Denver was especially hard hit because his mom had been his chief source of encouragement and hope. Now she was fading out of his life. He grew morose and seemed to get more comfort from those "undesirable" friends than Roy wanted to admit. Teresa seemed to bury her anguish in activities at the school.

Eventually it became clear that Becky would not live much longer. During the last few days the three family members took turns staying at her bedside. Denver wanted the middle of the night. He wanted to be there for her when others would not be there. They seemed to be able to communicate without words. Wrenching agonies competed with joyous prospects of a pain free future for his mom. Sometimes Roy would slip in and the two of them would chat softly about the years that had gone by. By now Denver had been out of school for nearly a year. Becky had achieved her wish of seeing her son graduate and then seemed to lose some of the will to live. Teresa struggled visibly, torn between the need to be at home and the desire to keep up with her many commitments at school. None of the three could find all the words they needed to share their feelings. Now where was God when we needed him?

Friends at the church, relatives and neighbors gave their support but Roy became mired in despair. The funeral was a difficult time. Denver blamed God for not helping them. Teresa avoided talking about it and Roy was at a loss of what to do. Many were the tributes and words of encouragement during those last days of her life and the weeks after the funeral but comfort for Roy was hard to find. Here he had been giving all these neat explanations, these formula solutions, these packaged answers to the problems of life and what did they do for him now? Was it all just a façade, an ego trip, a paper solution? What was any of that worth when it didn't give him or his family the answers they needed? Was everything he had been doing just a useless fake?

These memories were more than Roy could take at this point. He put the letter down, went to bed and cried himself to sleep.

In the morning Roy followed his usual pattern of spending some time in prayer. It was a real struggle to even keep his mind on track. It reminded him of the times that prayer and worship became topics of study for the two men from the plant. In his mind he replayed the time when they asked him about prayer. He wished that his prayers had kept his family together better. Reminders of the time Denver and Teresa told him they were moving flashed through his mind too.

Chapter 14:

Struggling With Prayer

Harry and Tom showed up for their regular small group study several weeks after the funeral, not knowing what to expect. They had not felt right about coming sooner but now had asked Roy to resume them. Roy admitted that he was in no shape to lead a study. Perhaps this time they should both just pray for him and the situation that had developed.

"I don't know how to pray publicly," objected Tom.
"I have real trouble with that too," declared Harry.
"What is the point of prayer anyway?" asked Tom. "If God knows everything why would we be telling him things in prayer? It doesn't make sense to me."
"I don't understand it all either, guys. I admit that sometimes my faith is challenged when prayer doesn't seem to change anything," responded Roy. "Think of it as a conversation with a very special and powerful friend. This 'friend' loves to hear from us, commands us to pray and promises to answer, though not always the way we had hoped."
"I've never had a friend like that," countered Harry.
"You do now," responded Roy. "Start by acknowledging his greatness and telling how much you appreciate what he has made and done for you."

"I guess we could think of something that fits that idea," said Tom.

"Then if you feel OK about it you can include admitting your weaknesses and fears to him. He understands and forgives."

"That is getting personal for sure," responded Harry in a guarded fashion.

"Don't feel compelled to do that here today but in private you may wish to do so at home. Then you can finish off with a few sentences expressing your requests for yourself and for others, especially me. That's not too difficult, is it?" asked Roy.

"Not for you but it is for us," remarked Harry.

"And now you expect us to pray?" objected Tom.

"Yes, I know how you feel, guys," moaned Roy. "I've been there many times. I'm there now."

"That's going to be tough for me," commented Harry.

"Me too," said Tom.

"If you did it anyway I would surely appreciate it because I'm in trouble," pleaded Roy.

"What if you start," ventured Tom, "and then we may each add a few words. What do you say, Harry?"

"Well, OK," he agreed.

Roy began in an impassioned way. It encouraged the others when their turn came to put in their plea too, complete with some faltering words of praise and confession and thanksgiving. Before the evening was over the three men had encircled each other with their arms and a few tears flowed. It may well have been that when Roy seemed most unable to lead the small group, he was most effective.

"Thanks a lot, guys," sighed Roy when they were finished. "This has meant a lot to me."

"Don't know if we really helped," responded Tom, "but I've learned something tonight."

"Yeah, I would never have dreamt that I'd ever pray out loud," exclaimed Harry. "We have learned something. This has been a unique experience."

"Guys, you have helped a lot, more than you could imagine. I've struggled with the idea of prayer too. Some time ago, during that puzzling time, I wrote out what I discovered about prayer. You can have a copy if you want," replied Roy.

"Sure," was the response of both of them. (Turn to Appendix 3 if you want to see a copy.)

They were both about to leave, but Harry was hesitating. "Guys," he sighed, "I've been struggling within myself about whether I should bring up this matter that is heavy on my heart, but I think I'd better share it with both of you. Roy, this will mean taking Tom into our confidence over the suspicions we've both had about some shady dealings at work. Is that OK with you?"

"Yes, definitely. The three of us have got to be a team. After all the Scripture reference about two or three being gathered together was about a meeting for prayer. This is where it needs to get practical. What's on your mind, Harry?"

"Let me fill Tom in on what's been troubling us. Not long ago Roy inspected an RV unit slated for referral to Kirk's shop for repair and found a number of hidden and weird false connections and adjustments that took only a short while for him to correct. He submitted a report that declared the RV fit for regular marketing but early the next morning Kirk came to haul it away after Jeb submitted a report that it was definitely deficient beyond our reasonable hope of quick repair. He declared it in need of greater expertise and confirmed that it be sent to Kirk for repairs. The problem is that he had only been at work for a few minutes and couldn't have even checked the RV out. We suspected foul play. I've done some checking and I believe we have a strong case."

"This could get ugly, Harry," replied Tom, with a sense of apprehension. "I've wondered about the number of RVs going to Kirk for expert repairs on items we supposedly couldn't fix, but how do we prove fraud? This is a risky venture."

"Here's the scoop, guys. I had to work in the office for a bit on a matter that included the repair referral files. There have been 7 of them in the last 10 months. This last one shows a 6 hour 'search and rescue' type of job from 8:00 to 3:00 on the day Kirk picked it up. Jeb arrived just after 7:30 that morning and the RV was hooked up and out of there before 8:00 a.m. Jeb could not have done any valid inspection to over-rule Roy's work in those few minutes. However, a report from him is on file declaring the RV as needing expert services and Roy's report is missing. I suspect that neither Jeb nor Kirk did any work on the RV and simply submitted a fraudulent bill. I also suspect that most of the previous ones were similar rip-offs. Is it time for us to blow the whistle on someone?"

"You mean my report has been taken out?" asked Roy.

"Yes."

"What do you recommend as the next step?"

"I think the three of us need to go see the General Manager privately and lay it all out for him. We'd tell him that we'd be willing to testify if needed. It would be his move next."

The three of them discussed the pros and cons of poking their noses into this matter, knowing the possible ugly battle that could result. They resorted to a time of prayer and then come to the united conclusion that it was their Christian duty to act.

Chapter 15

The Trap

"Roy, how are you doing?" asked Barb, the office administrator. "I'm so sorry about what happened to Becky. It must be really tough for you."

"It's not fun, that's for sure."

"How can I be of help?"

"I'm getting along OK. Our son and daughter are picking up some of the pieces. The church family is supportive and in spite of it all, the Lord is good."

"I know a little bit about what it's like to be single," winced Barb, seemingly steering the conversation away from the religious part of it. "It can get lonely."

"Yah, you're right about that."

"Roy, I want to be there for you if I can ever help. OK?"

"OK, thanks, Barb."

The interaction left Roy wondering. On the one hand he was perplexed about why Barb had suddenly taken such an interest in his well-being when for the first few months she had hardly even said hello to him. Then again, Becky hadn't died before this either. The attention was a bit heart-warming even though there were some caution signals faintly beeping in the background.

Cinnamon buns began to appear for him from Barb during that week. Roy ended up being sent or called to the office a couple of times on seemingly trivial matters. Each time Barb would heap attention and warmth on him. Then she asked Roy if he would be willing to stop in at her place to check out a washing machine that wasn't working right. Would he look at it first to see if she really needed to call in an expensive repairman? Roy could hardly say no after all she had done for him but it bothered him that he might end up alone in a single woman's home in the evening. He decided to confide in Harry.

"I smell a rat," concluded Harry after Roy filled him in on what had been happening. "I have not had a good impression of Barb's character and this doesn't look good."

"What do I do now? I can't very well say that I won't help when she's been giving me things. It's not like I'm consorting with someone else's wife. However, from what you say she's not a Christian. I have no plans of pursuing this as a relationship. Maybe she's setting some sort of a trap for me."

"There is a way to test that."

"What's that?"

"Take another man with you. If it displeases her you have your answer."

"Good idea. Would you be that guy?"

"I was afraid you'd say that. Guess I'd better be available. By the way, don't be too sure that she is as single as she claims. I've seen her with Kirk quite often."

"With Kirk!"

"Yup. You know what? This could get really interesting."

Roy and Harry showed up at Barb's place at the appointed time. She beamed when she answered the door for Roy, but her expression turned sour when she spotted Harry.

"I brought Harry along because he's got some skills in this field that I don't have, but mostly because I made this personal commitment to Becky about not being alone with another woman in her house. It's still with me."

Barb was dressed in rather suggestive attire. Roy was glad Harry had come along.

After an awkward silence Roy asked, "Could we look at the washing machine?"

"Ya, sure. It's right this way."

A few minutes inspection revealed a bolt that had presumably "worked itself loose" and was lying on the bottom. With that done, the two left, with Barb attempting to be thankful.

In the car Harry muttered, "That had a not-so-hidden agenda written all over it, Roy."

"Even I could see that, Harry. Thanks for being there for me. You are a wise man."

"I've got an idea, Roy. Pull over just a bit down the street where the car will be out of sight. Then we'll walk back in the shadows behind that tree and watch the house. I have a suspicion we'll see something interesting."

They did just that and within a minute a man was seen approaching Barb in that same front room right in front of the big window.

"Do you recognize that man, Roy?"

"No I don't. She said she was single. What is he doing there?"

"That guy is Kirk. And look what he's carrying."

"It's a camera. Are you suggesting that he was hoping to get a picture of me in that house with Barb?"

"Not just any picture, Roy. A really hot and juicy one would suit them just fine for blackmail. I think Barb is in on this shady business that's going on and she's been assigned to silence you somehow. They must know that you've smelled a rat and they are running scared. I don't think their plan would have worked, Roy, but they might have found a way to make you look bad. You know, Christian and all."

"Harry, I feel sick. I was being sucked in. It's just like the devil to use a low blow when you're already feeling down. You've been a lifesaver, Harry."

"That's what Christian brothers are for, aren't they. Also, Roy, I owe you a lot. Let's go. This case is getting really interesting. We'll delve into this some more on Thursday night, OK?"

"Sure, Harry. I need the support you guys give me."

Chapter 16

Facing Crucial Issues

The men were a bit more relaxed at their next meeting. Harry and Roy filled Tom in on what had developed at Barb's house a few nights ago. Together they laid plans for how they would approach Todd, the General Manager, with the information they had assembled so far. It was decided that Harry would approach him with a short briefing on their suspicions and ask for a meeting of the three of them with him. They sought the Lord in prayer about it, building on what they had done about prayer the previous week. It was just what they needed in order to see the practical value of prayer.

"Last week you really helped us overcome a hurdle that has been plaguing us for weeks, Roy. It was the whole idea of praying out loud. Sure was appropriate tonight too," commented Harry.

"Yes," added Tom. "I had no idea prayer could be this practical."

"There's another issue I am struggling with," stated Harry.

"What would that be?" asked Roy.

"I hear the words 'worship service' quite often when church people talk, but I don't really understand what worship is all about," deplored Harry.

"Me neither," added Tom. "Got any thoughts on that one?"

"I've wrestled with that one too. It is not an easy topic. It has a lot to do with how committed you are to what you believe in. It takes a strong faith in someone or something to worship. However, it is fairly obvious that mankind has a built in need to worship something," explained Roy. "Whether we admit it or not we all commit ourselves to something or someone, even if it is only ourselves. In a sense we actually become like what we worship."

"You mean that a person whose life is all bound up in following a movie star or a rock star or some athlete is worshiping that person?" asked Tom.

"Yes, I would say that is possible. A Christian needs to be committed to Jesus in a significant way if there is to be any genuine worship."

"That makes it sound like enjoying something means you are worshiping it."

"To just enjoy something or someone is a step below worship. Worship comes from the idea of worth-ship. It places that person or activity as pre-eminent in your thinking and something or someone to whom your loyalty and adoration are a priority."

"So you figure that a person can get to the place where a sport or an entertainment can be the object of worship," declared Tom.

"'Fraid so," answered Roy. "The Bible says we must worship the Lord and serve him only. He is very firm on that. Granting worship to something or someone else is idolatry. Worship is not a ritual, it is a lifestyle. A Christian's faith is legitimately a target for the opposition if that person claims to worship God but is obviously investing most of the time, abilities, money and energy into something else."

"So how do you worship? What does it look like?" asked Harry.

"I once collected a lot of verses from the Bible on that subject and then put them into six piles according to what was happening in each one. Then I chose one or two representative verses in each pile and gave each pile a label. To make it easier for me to remember I made each label name start with the letter A. Want to know the result? I can give you a copy."

"Sure," agreed Tom. That's what we came for."

Roy fetched a copy for each of them and together they worked through its content.

(Appendix 4 is that copy, if you want to know what it says.)

"If we observe these things we will be genuine worshipers in our actions and prayers," concluded Roy.

"That's another huge assignment," objected Tom. "I can't live up to that."

"None of us can in our own strength, Tom, but we can grow in our ability to do it."

"There's just so much to the Christian life that I hadn't thought of before," added Harry. "We're going to have to really address this one personally."

The two men took a copy home for further study.

The next evening Denver and Teresa approached Roy with the intent of informing their dad that final plans for leaving were now in place. Denver had graduated two years ago and was working for a local builder as a carpentry apprentice. Teresa had just graduated and was heading for university.

"Dad," began Denver, "Teresa and I have been talking about our plans for leaving this town. Teresa wants to live near the university she'll be attending on her scholarship and I hope to find a job in carpentry somewhere in the same area.

I need a change from being around here. It holds too many unpleasant memories."

"That means we will both be leaving at the end of August," added Teresa.

Roy paused for a bit, looked down at the floor and then at the two of them. "I can understand why you would do that. It'll be terribly lonely without you but I knew the time would come for this. You made that clear a while ago. It'll be really tough, losing mom and now both of you."

"Dad, you're not losing us. We are still alive!" responded Teresa.

"So we'll keep in touch, won't we? Then I won't feel as lost."

"Definitely, yes," promised Denver.

"What are your prospects, Denver?" asked Roy.

"Two other guys from this town want to do the same thing. We'll try to find a place where we can stay together to cut down on expenses and so that we're not alone."

Roy knew who those other two would likely be and was apprehensive about where this would lead. He also knew the added challenges to faith that Teresa would face in university. In all, the future did not look that bright for what was left of his family.

"Look, I want to help both of you," offered Roy. "Teresa, we've already worked out how I will help you financially and I want to do something for Denver too."

"You don't have to, dad," objected Denver.

"But I want to. Suppose we work something out so that you know what to expect."

When the details were finalized the three of them went to bed, but Roy couldn't get to sleep for a long time. He kept thinking of what was ahead for him and his two children, though now he had to think of them as adults out on their own. It tore away at his heart.

Roy recalled how he had tried to put his own circumstances out of his mind by getting into a discussion or debate with Sam. It brought him back to some of those more joyful days when he experienced some victories in the workplace.

Chapter 17

More Critical Issues

"Hey, Sam, wait up!" called Roy when he spotted him downtown that Saturday afternoon. "I've been thinking and I'd like to run some ideas past you because I know that you are a thinking man too. What do you say it's my turn to buy coffee?"

"OK, I've got some time so why not," responded Sam. "What's on your mind?"

"It's occurred to me that everyone looks at life through his or her own set of lenses and filters. It's like each person's perception of what's real is determined by the lenses he/she looks through and the filters he/she uses to screen information. Some have rose-colored lenses and everything looks better than it really is. Some have distorted lenses, some are out of focus, some are dark or whatever. Some people's filters are preset to screen out things that should be included. Other filters let things through that should be filtered out. Does that sound logical to you?"

"Hey, slow down a bit. You're really piling on the philosophy and logic."

They entered the coffee shop. "What can I get you, Sam," asked Roy, "double double?"

"Just down my line, Roy."

They found a table for two in a corner and revisited the conversation.

"That concept I referred to has been labeled the person's worldview. It's what he/she deems to be real, important and true."

"So, what's you're point?"

"I think there's a fairly simple way to determine what a person's worldview is?"

"You really think so? Is this another one of your cut and dried acronyms? Or maybe they all start with the same letter and you've got it all in a neatly packaged solution."

"No, no acronym, no alliteration, just five simple questions. They are profoundly simple, yet simply profound."

"Oh my. That is clever. It might even solve all the world's problems. OK, enough put-downs. I'll listen to your gems. What are those questions?"

"I believe that the answers to these five questions determine the kind of lens a person is looking through and the kind of filters being used. In turn that defines a person's worldview. Here they are.

1. How did everything that exists get here, including us?
2. Why are we here?
2. What went wrong?
4. How do we fix it?
5. When we die is there life after that death?

I believe these are the basic questions that people everywhere have been asking for centuries. What do you think?"

"Well, they are common philosophical concerns. I guess lots of people have wrestled with them. I rather suspect that many have never even thought about what lens or filter they are using? Would we consider them blind?"

"Their worldview shows in their priorities even if they themselves don't see it or have not deliberately dealt with the questions. They show what's important to them by the way they live even if they can't put it into words."

"How's that?"

"Some live for fun and money. Some are driven to achieve and don't care about moral issues. Some hold to high standards of integrity. These will show in how they live."

"So what?"

"Let's consider two extremes in the kind of answers people could give. Take the first question. The atheistic evolutionist would say that either we came from nothing or else some eternally self-existent primeval slime had the potential to develop into all that exists. The Big Bang theory claims that nothingness condensed into a small spot and exploded with the result that the atoms coalesced into all the billion of stars and all the planets including earth. From there evolution produced life and all the species we have. The monotheistic creationist would say that it was designed by an Intelligent Being of great power who is eternally self-existent. Then there are multitudes of philosophies and ideologies in between those two. Which one you believe will show in how you live."

"Not every atheist is morally corrupt and not every creationist is morally upright. I can't accept a dichotomous conclusion here."

"But the answer to that first question has to affect the person. Whether you believe or don't believe that there is a Higher Power you are accountable to, will affect your lifestyle and how you make decisions."

"OK. Keep going."

"If a person believes that we came out of nowhere by chance there is no possibility of having a purpose for our existence. If we've been created by a Designer, there is a purpose. Our Creator tells us what the purpose is when he says that the most important thing is to love God with all our heart, mind, soul and strength. He adds that the second most important thing is to love others as ourselves. Then there are many ideas about purpose between those two extremes."

"People can create their own purpose in life," argued Sam.

"Exactly," agreed Roy. "And when people do, it is not the purpose that God set out. That's the problem."

"Maybe."

"When we get to number three it is logical that if there is no purpose there can be no wrong either. Right or wrong is based on either meeting or missing a purpose. This also declares that there is nothing to fix if there is no such thing as wrong. That takes care of number four. For the evangelical creationist sin is what's wrong and Jesus' death on the cross provides the solution. I know that the world is full of all kinds of philosophies and ideas on what's wrong and how to fix it that are not like either one of those two extremes. But whatever a person does believe in shapes his/her worldview."

"I've got to think on that one, Roy."

"We've already talked a bit about the last one, namely what happens when we die. The atheistic evolutionist would say we go back to nothingness. There is nothing after death. The evangelical creationist will say that we either go to be with the Lord in heaven or with Satan in hell. In between there again is a plethora of beliefs. What do you think, Sam?"

"I don't know but I don't go for either extreme. I believe there is something but what it's like we'll just have to wait and see. I believe it is more positive than negative."

"So what's your worldview based on those five questions, Sam?"

"I said I'll have to think about it. Don't push it, Roy!"

"OK, OK. I'll ease off. I'd be glad to listen to your assessment when you're ready."

"I'll tell you if I ever get that far. Meanwhile, I gotta go. See you later."

When Roy pulled into the driveway at home he spotted Denver sitting on the front steps, waiting. Roy banged his forehead with his own fist and slumped into a bit of despair. He had done it again. He had promised to be back in a few minutes to pick up Denver so that the two of them could go on a hike, and now he was at least half an hour late. It was likely to be their last hike together for a while.

"Denver, I'm sorry to keep you waiting. I got distracted in town but that is not an excuse. Let's go right away and I'll try to make it up to you."

"It's OK, dad," mumbled Denver, but Roy could tell that it wasn't. The afternoon didn't turn out as well as it was supposed to.

Sometime after the two had moved out Roy found himself very involved in that risky whistle-blowing case they had undertaken.

"Say, Harry, what's happening about setting up that meeting with Todd?' asked Roy as the three men sat down for their weekly group session.

"I gave him a brief summary of the suspicions we have, but he was not willing to set a meeting time. I get the feeling he either wants to proceed with caution or maybe not pursue it at all," answered Harry.

"Should we just give up the idea?" asked Tom.

"Not yet,' responded Harry. "We just need to be patient. I'll let you guys know as soon as anything definite develops. Meanwhile I get the feeling that another bash at praying about it wouldn't be a bad idea."

"Right, that'll be our first priority tonight," agreed Roy. "Then we'll move into whatever questions or concerns you may have."

After the three of them expressed themselves in refreshingly simple and candid prayer, Roy asked what might be of concern for them this time.

"Some time ago you told us about the importance of worship," recalled Harry. "You implied that Christians need to get together as a church to worship. Can't we just do that on our own? Why would we have to be part of a church? There's so much trouble associated with them."

"There are horrible stories associated with the church," admitted Roy, "but there are also great opportunities and glorious experiences. Remember that a church is made up of people, not a building. If, at a campfire, you remove one coal and set it off to one side what will happen to it?"

"It'll soon quit burning and get cold," declared Tom.

"That's what happens to Christians who try to go it alone. We need each other's support and challenge. Not one of us is equipped to do all that is needed to be built up in our faith. We need others and they need us."

"How do you know that?" asked Harry.

"If we had the opportunity to hear from someone who had committed his life to planting churches at great personal sacrifice and danger, would that convince us? Suppose after years of experience he shared with us his final words of advice, would we want to listen?"

"I guess that would be a good idea," agreed Tom.

"We have such an account from the Apostle Paul in Acts chapter 20. From what I can deduce from his meeting with the church leaders of Ephesus he emphasized four things that the church needs to be doing.

a. A commitment to serve the Lord and honor Him – that's **worship**;
b. A desire to grow stronger in how we live the Christian life – that's our **walk** with the Lord, namely how we live from day to day;
c. A need to tell others about the Lord – that's our **witness,** sharing our faith with others; and

d. A plan to help those in need inside or outside the church – that's our **work** of compassion for those in need.

These four things can best be accomplished by working together as a team. That is what the church is about. That is why the Bible assumes Christians will meet together as well as doing those things that will help them grow as individuals. We gather to worship and learn. We scatter to witness and serve."

The three of them hashed the subject through and through for the next hour. After they had done that, Harry was more convinced than ever that they needed to act on the fraud that was happening because it was part of Christian duty, part of the work Christians should do.
"Roy, what you told us about the purpose of the church tells me we need to stand up for what's right, doesn't it?" asked Harry.
"Yes, it does."
"Then we can't just stand by knowing that there are crooked schemes being perpetrated on the company by a conspiracy of some workers, can we? We've got to be insistent."
"You mean we need to convince Todd to listen," mused Roy.
"It's unpleasant and a bit risky but do we have a choice?"
Roy paused to think a bit. He had not counted on this practical an application of what they had been discussing in their small group. The three of them tossed the issue back and forth for a while with Harry being the more insistent one that something had to be done.
"I know Todd a bit," offered Harry. "I believe I could get that appointment with him for the three of us without being too pushy. What do you say I keep trying?"

Tom and Roy agreed to this plan. Two days later he motioned the two of them off to one side after work and shared the results.

"It's on for Thursday after work," said Harry. "We will make our way home, or at least pretend to, but instead meet at my place. From there we will come back to the plant where Todd, the General Manager, will be waiting for us in his office. We won't come back until it's pretty clear that everyone else has left."

"What are we going to say to him?" asked Roy.

"We'll simply tell him the facts we know, and the implications that we strongly suspect. He will likely ask questions. He may even have the company's legal counsel present. Just be very clear and honest in your answers. We have nothing to hide and no personal gain at stake. We especially want to be clear that there is no feeling of revenge or vendetta involved. We are there to expose fraudulent activity against the company."

"OK. Thursday it is," agreed Tom.

"I'll be there," promised Roy.

In Todd's office Harry acted as spokesperson and laid out the facts to Todd.

"This is a serious allegation we are making, Todd," began Harry. "We have no personal benefit of any kind at stake here, just fair play for the company. We believe the company is being cheated by a small group of employees who are gaining financially by it."

"Do you realize the position you are putting yourself in?" warned Todd. "If this turns out to be unfounded you'll be the ones in deep trouble. Whistleblowers have been known to be treated like dirt or worse. Have you done your homework thoroughly? As you can see, I've got Ted, our legal counsel here, who'll know if we have a case."

"We hesitated for quite a while before even considering this, Todd. It would be easier for us just to continue turning a blind eye to what we are sure is happening. That would make us morally an accomplice if we did nothing. We'll tell you what we know and from there it is up to you. We do not plan to press charges. That would have to come from you if you feel they are valid."

"OK, go ahead."

"The company has an agreement with Kirk to repair any units that defy the expertise of our men to diagnose or remedy. Right?"

"Yes, that is correct."

"David, the Sales Manager, authorizes the inspection and consequent assignment to Kirk of any unit deemed deficient in this way by one of our men who work on that aspect of the RV. Right?"

"Right."

"There have been an inordinate number funneled in that direction, all of them authorized by David, inspected by Jeb and clerically processed by Barbara, who is Kirk's live-in partner."

"That's a set-up for fraudulent activity alright, but only circumstantial. It doesn't prove anything," warned Ted, the legal counsel.

"There's more to this," declared Harry. "I'll ask Roy to explain."

"You are right about that," agreed Roy, "there is more. A few weeks ago a unit came to us for inspection by Jeb but he was away that day so Gary asked me to do it. I found some very unusual, hidden bad connections and faulty adjustments which took only a short while to correct once I spotted them. I submitted my report to Gary and to the office where Barb works. Early the next morning I noted Kirk hauling that same unit away. Jeb had only been at work a few minutes but had turned in a deficiency verification to Gary and to the office. He couldn't have even checked it out in that time."

Harry continued, "I had occasion to file another report two weeks ago and in the process noticed that Jeb's report was there, but Roy's had been removed. What does that tell you?"

"You're saying that uncalled for repair referrals are being made with David, Barb, Jeb and Kirk in collusion."

"Attached to Jeb's report was a copy of the bill for Kirk's repairs. It came to $843.47, showing itemized parts and labor. We would guess that none of that work was done and none of those parts were ever supplied," declared Harry.

"How could we prove that?" asked Todd.

"You could start by requiring invoices for the parts ordered and even by cross-examining the mechanics in his shop. Perhaps their records of who worked on what jobs the days they had the RV would be conclusive information as to whether anyone worked on it at all."

"We're sorry to load this onto you, Todd," offered Roy, "but it's up to you from here on. If you choose not to follow up on this we will at least have a clear conscience. If you pursue it, we will be there for you."

"OK, guys. I've got to really think this one through. Thanks, sort of."

"That's not all, Todd,' interjected Harry. "After I discovered the missing file Barb began to become overly friendly and concerned about Roy. As you know he lost his wife a while ago. Barb said nothing then but now has been showing compassion, asking how he's doing, bringing him goodies for his meals and seeking to get him to come over to her house. I'll let Roy take it from here."

"She asked me to help her by coming to the house to check out the washing machine which wasn't working properly. She said she was alone and didn't know what to do. Would I check it out before she called the repairman?"

"Both Harry and I have seen her together with Kirk a number of times around town," volunteered Tom. "Why wouldn't she call him. He's an appliance expert."

"I felt obligated to help but uneasy about going so I confided in Harry. The result was that we decided to go together to avoid any appearance of questionable behavior on my part. She wasn't happy when she saw that Harry was with me."

"She was wearing a frown but not much else," commented Harry.

"The problem with the machine turned out to be a bolt that had come loose. After we left Harry suggested that we park out of sight and walk back under a tree where we could see the front window. Sure enough, Kirk appeared, obviously agitated and carrying a camera," continued Roy. "We believe it was a set-up. I think they wanted to trap me into an immoral act that Kirk would photograph and blackmail me with. He knew that my image in the community and the church would be a powerful psychological ploy he could use to silence me because they must have become aware somehow that we were onto what they were doing."

"This is getting dicey and spicy," exclaimed Todd.

"If we're going to do something it should be soon because I think they are onto us in spite of us trying to keep it quiet. It's in your court, Todd," declared Harry.

"OK, guys. I've got the picture. Give us a little time to absorb the implications and think of a plan of action. I'll call you if I need you. Meanwhile mums the word."

The next day Todd, accompanied by the company's legal counsel, went to Kirk's shop.

"Kirk, I've got some questions about that last job you did for us," began Todd.

"What's that matter?" asked Kirk, "Isn't the unit working right?"

"It's working just fine."

"Then what's the problem?"

"The day before you picked it up Roy worked on it and got it into top shape. When Jeb came in the next morning he simply reversed the report, removed Roy's and let you pick it up anyway."

"He did what?" exclaimed Kirk. "He told me he had checked it out."

"What did you find when you worked on it?" demanded Todd.

"Well, you got the invoice, didn't you?"

"Yes, we did, and now I'd like to see verification of the parts ordered for that RV job plus the time card record of the person who worked on it."

Kirk's face blanched and he stumbled over his words. "Well, I'll need some time to dig those out."

"No, you don't need time. We'll just go in right now and find them, if they exist."

"You can't just come into my office and demand that!" retorted Kirk.

"Our legal counsel, Ted here, has got things lined up for an on the spot search warrant if you want to challenge me on this one. There are no invoices for those parts, are there? And the time cards will show that all your men had worked on other jobs during the whole time that the RV was in the shop, right?"

There was no answer from Kirk.

"Kirk, you've been defrauding us," demanded Todd.

Kirk still gave no answer.

"How many other jobs did you bill us for without doing any significant work on them?"

Kirk just shrugged his shoulders.

"You have a choice, Kirk. Either you come clean with us now or face a court trial. Our legal counsel will start action immediately unless you come up with the answers. We'll demand the same invoices on every job you did for us during the last year. It would be best to settle it now without all the legal hassle," reasoned Todd.

"Awright, awright," growled Kirk. "There have been five others."

"Here's the scoop, Kirk. We believe that Jeb, David and Barb are in cahoots with you. If that is the case, here is how you can avoid prosecution. Each one of the four of you who have benefited financially are to reimburse the company the full amount you took plus legal costs. Dig out the invoices on those five so that we know the exact amounts. After that you've got just a few days to repay before we launch a court case. Is that clear?"

"Yah, I guess so." Kirk had little choice in the matter.

Gary was filled in as to what was happening at a meeting the next day called by Todd for Gary with Roy, Harry and Tom present. He was challenged as to what he might already have known about the situation. Gary became nervous and agitated.

"What's the problem, Gary?" asked Todd.

"I..I did know something was not right but when I started to question it David blackmailed me. You see, I made a big, really big mistake nearly two years ago and they've held me over a barrel ever since with threats of telling on me."

"Care to tell us about it, Gary?" asked Roy.

"Only if you guarantee to keep it confidential. I can't afford to have this slip out some other way, although one of those three might do it anyway."

They all agreed to the conditions.

"Almost two years ago Barb got me to come to her house and seduced me. I was easy pickings because things weren't going well between my wife and me. She'd been all warmth and sort of caring toward me for a while and then this happened. After that they used it as a blackmail threat when I questioned those shady transactions. They said they would tell my wife. They also forced me to find a way to move Roy out of that crew."

Gary practically broke down as he turned to face Roy.

"Roy, I've felt terrible about what I accused you of especially since it was so close to Becky's death. I caved in to David because of his threats. I'm really sorry about the grief I caused you. I know you didn't deserve it. I was confused about the whole thing. I feel awful. Now what do I do?"

Harry and Roy looked at each other knowingly. "That explains a lot, Gary. You are right that I couldn't figure out what was going on. It seemed so out of place. But I forgive you. And as for Barb, she tried that on me too," said Roy, "but Harry came with me to the house for a supposed washing machine repair. That cut her off."

"You guys were smart, I wasn't."

Roy made a suggestion. "Todd, suppose the three of us were to commit to be there for Gary as he seeks to work this one out. You probably don't want to get into this one anyway."

"You got it, Roy. It's all yours for sure."

In the morning Todd called in David, Barb and Jeb separately.

"What's up, Todd?" asked Jeb.

"The jig's up, Jeb," responded Todd in a matter of fact way.

"What do you mean?"

"The scheme you and David and Barb and Kirk have been using is finished," declared Todd.

"What scheme?" asked Jeb, feigning innocence.

"We've gathered the evidence, nailed down the records on the jobs done and conclusively found that six of the RV 'repairs' sent to Kirk were fraudulent. All of them were authorized by David, inspected by you, processed by Barb and handled by Kirk. The jig is over. Kirk has admitted it and you know your part in it."

"It was David's idea. He offered me $100 to $150 for each one. Why shouldn't I get in on the money?"

"It's dishonest. It's stealing. Worst of all it means we can't trust you. Jeb you're through here. We'll give you the opportunity to settle out of court on this one. Ted, our legal counsel, is here and can set that up with you right now. If you choose to challenge this in court you may but I can tell you now that you won't win and it will cost you more money plus a criminal record. When you go you'll find all your own tools and belongings beside your truck. You're through here. Hope you learn from this."

Jeb was stunned after meeting with Ted, stomped out of the office, slammed his truck door and roared out of the lot.

Barb was next. She already knew what was coming since Kirk had told her. She tried to give excuses.

"Kirk's company was in bad financial shape so we needed some quick cash last year so we agreed to David's plan. It worked so easily that we kept doing it. It wasn't that big a deal. There isn't a lot of money involved and the company hardly notices it. Can't we work something out?"

"I need an office administrator I can trust. You've lost that. You have the opportunity to settle out of court. Ted, our legal counsel, is in the next room. You can refuse to accept our offer and challenge it in court but you'll end up in even worse shape that way. Get all your personal belongings together and go. I wish I didn't have to do this." Barb left sullenly.

David was different case.

"Todd, it's not that big a deal. What's a few thousand for this company? They're not paying us enough to begin with. We're just getting our share."

"And you are a church person? Is this kind of stealing OK in your ethics? That's what makes you so-called Christians stink in my estimation. And then forcing a transfer of Roy by manipulating Gary to move him! How low can you get – using blackmail. David, you're getting the same treatment as the other three. Get your personal belongings and go. Ted is waiting to offer an out of court settlement to you. Consider that generous. A court case would leave you in worse shape so I advise you to accept this offer. Furthermore, Roy and Gary are going to work out this issue of Gary's moral unfaithfulness with Barb. You stay out of that. If you mess with him I'll go public about you. Do you understand?

David sat there in stunned silence.

"Just get out of here! You disgust me!" declared Todd. David left.

"I remember the day Teresa and I told you that we were moving out. I know it came as a bit of a blow to you, but I just had to do it. I also know that you wanted us home for Thanksgiving but right now I've got other plans. I still have a picture of that chat in my mind. It was a turning point for all of us, I guess. Well, we'll come home some other time for a visit. Bye."

Again Roy replayed the departure scene in his mind.

Chapter 18

Surprises

Roy remembered settling down with the newspaper, and trying to erase the memories of the conflict at work, when Denver and Teresa walked in.

"Dad," asked Denver, "can we talk for a bit?"

"Sure," responded Roy with eagerness, "love to chat."

I've given my boss notice at work about the day on which I finish here. Like I said earlier, there are too many unpleasant memories here," replied Denver.

"Oooo! I'm sorry to hear that but I guess I knew it was coming. We had talked about this some time ago. Where exactly are you thinking of going?" Not another downer, please, thought Roy.

"Couple of guys and I are heading out to a job not far from where Teresa will be at university. I'll move her stuff there at the same time that I go."

"It'll be good for us to be able to get together occasionally," added Teresa.

"I see" murmured Roy. "It'll sure be lonely here but it's logical that this would happen. Sounds like you've already got something lined up, Denver."

"Yeah, the two guys I mentioned, Sid and Del, know a construction fellow up there who needs workers. They also have located an apartment that the three of us can share. I'll get you all the details and we can stay in touch."

Roy couldn't help the sigh that escaped. The two guys Denver mentioned were not the ones he would want as Denver's buddies but it seemed like they were among the few who had included Denver in their circle at school and at work. Interfering would not help the matter. Denver was now 20.

"That's appreciated, son," said Roy. "I was fully willing to bring Teresa there myself, though."

"It's alright, dad" offered Teresa. "You could come up after I'm settled in and see me and the place I'm in. Since Denver is going up anyway in his car it won't be necessary for you to bring me there."

"OK. Guess not."

Roy couldn't help but be a little disappointed that he was left out of this major transition. He'd have to make the goodbye scene at home as meaningful as he could without letting the discouragement show. His apprehensions were accentuated by the drift he couldn't help but notice in Teresa's spiritual life.

"Teresa, maybe this would be a good time to chat about a few final arrangements regarding what you will take with you from the house. We can also delve into tying down the final financial arrangements that we planned a while ago."

"I've got most of it figured out already."

"I really would like to go over that with you so that I'm clear on the big picture."

"Well, OK. I'll get the sheet on which I've planned it all. Be back in a minute."

Denver looked a bit uneasy as Teresa left and only the two of them were in the room. Roy sensed that and decided to relieve the tension.

"Denver, you have every right to do what you are doing. I will support you and pray for you. You don't have to feel obligated to be here for me. True, it will be an adjustment for me but that's an inevitable event."

"Well, I kind of sensed that you aren't completely happy about the decision."

"You're good at reading people, son. It's true that I have some reservations about the influence of Sid and Del on your life. That's an issue you have to deal with. How do you think it will affect your commitment as a Christian?"

"I dunno, dad."

"It won't be easy but it could be the character building experience you need. I'm there for you anytime you want to chat, son."

"OK, dad. I'll remember that."

Teresa came in with her plans and Denver left.

"You do have this worked out to a T," commented Roy after reading her sheet. "You are so well-organized and astute about almost everything."

"Why did you say 'almost everything'?"

"You did catch me on that, didn't you," chuckled Roy. "What father doesn't have some apprehensions when his daughter heads off to university?"

"I'll be just fine, dad."

"Yes, you have it together. You do so many things well and I'm sure you'll do well there too. Certainly the scholarships you were awarded have made things go hugely better for my wallet. My concern is that sometimes a person's strengths become the entry point for their greatest weakness."

"What? I don't get it. How can that be?"

"Take the example of the wisest foolish man that ever lived. His strong points became the doorway for his downfall."

"You must be talking about Solomon."

"Yes."

"I'm not a king or a queen, neither am I rich like he was. I don't think the comparison is valid."

"On that level, no, but on another level it is valid for all of us. You see, even though he was privileged with unique abilities and closeness to God at first, we are told that the time came when he wanted *'to see what was worthwhile for men to do under heaven during the few days of their lives.'* That's a quote from Ecclesiastes 2:3. He already had responsibilities and opportunities to be fully involved in the most worthwhile life available but he wanted to look elsewhere. Brilliant minds are curious and searching. That's you."

"I don't know if I'm that brilliant, but, yes, I am searching and curious about what life is really about."

"Teresa, I respect you're desire to search. I suppose it's a must in the growing up process. May I offer the following for you to include in your thinking as you search?"

"Well, alright, but is this going to be another one of your cut and dried, alliterated, acronym or acrostic sermons?"

"Are they that bad?"

"If you use them too often they are annoying."

"I try to use them only if I want to have something that is easier for me to remember. I don't force the pattern when it doesn't really fit."

"Anyway, go ahead."

Roy cleared his throat and began with some apprehension.

"According to the rest of that chapter in Ecclesiastes, Solomon tried four things in his search for worthwhile things to do. First he undertook great projects and surrounded himself with a mass of possessions. He concluded that was meaningless and a chasing after the wind.

Second, he went for pleasure, including many wives and concubines. Same result.

Third, he pursued achievements and became *'greater by far than anyone in Jerusalem'*. Again he assessed that as meaningless chasing after the wind.

Last, he turned his thoughts to consider wisdom and the influence it would bring to his fame. Same conclusion. In fact, the assessment was so disappointing that in 2:17 he makes the astonishing statement: '*So I hated life.*'"

"Do you really think I'm going to do the same thing? Are you worried that I'll become a prostitute on campus? Dad, this is not fair!!"

"No, Teresa, you have standards and I appreciate that. What I will say is that everyone on earth is naturally inclined to make one or more of those four things the major motivator in his/her life. This is not aimed at you as a target. This is for everyone, including me."

"So what do you think I'm going for?"

"Achievement and influence."

"What's wrong with that?"

"They're only wrong if they take first place. All four of those are valid in everyone's life. Everyone has something of all four of them and that is good as long as none of them take first priority."

"And I guess I don't need to ask what should take first priority!"

"No, you would know what I'd say. But it doesn't really matter what I'd say. It matters what Jesus said was most important. In Mark 12:29 – 31 he made that very clear. The most important thing is our relationship with God and the second one is our relationship with people. The choice we have to make is whether the things we own, the activities we enjoy, the achievements we accomplish and the influences we wield are there to enhance our relationships or whether we are going to try to use God and people to enhance any of those four for ourselves. Put simply the choice is whether we will use God and people to get these things or whether we will use these things to relate better to God and people."

"Dad, I'm hung up on the basis for all this. You quote Scripture as a final authority. Yet, from what I've learned, the contents of the Bible are a collection of writings and letters that people have put together and a group of guys decided which ones would be considered God's Word. They are just human documents that contain a lot of good ideas but who can really say that they are God's Word?"

"It is a question of faith, but not blind faith. The Scriptures have proved themselves."

"I'm not convinced about that. Other philosophies and religions have worthwhile things to say too. Not only that, this whole business of eternal punishment and Jesus being the only way out doesn't seem right. On top of that, the first few chapters in Genesis read like a myth and seem most unscientific. I don't get all these fairytale miracles the Bible contains. I just have a hard time believing all that stuff."

"You've heard plenty from me before on how the theory of evolution outstrips all the miracles of the Bible put together if you want to talk about fairytale myths."

"Yes, I know, dad, and you've made some very strong points there. I just have to get this all straight in my head somehow."

"You are right. You do have to do that. I'll be praying for you."

"OK, dad. I gotta go."

"Sure, Teresa. Love you, dear. And by the way, you can remember those four things by calling them possessions, pleasure, power and prestige."

"You just can't give up, dad!"

"Had to put that in," laughed Roy.

Roy finished reading the letter from Denver for the umpteenth time, then sat down aimlessly in the rocking chair.

The phone was ringing. Roy felt a bit reluctant about answering it since so many of the calls meant reliving events. Would this be another well-meaning person wanting to do something or say something to help without really knowing what to do or say? The answering machine clicked in. It was

Celeste, one of the ladies in the weekly Care Group that he and Becky had attended. Yesterday the group had met in Celeste's home but Roy hadn't come. Roy almost picked up the phone, but didn't. Celeste expressed the concern of the group, mentioning how they missed Roy and hoped that he would let them know if there was something they could do to help. Roy remembered how Celeste, a widow Becky's age, had been such a great friend to Becky. Roy sensed a yearning to talk to her but just couldn't bring himself to attempt it in his current depressed state.

Then the phone rang again. This time he picked it up right away. Maybe she was calling again, but it was Denver. Roy's face brightened. After a few pleasantries and inquiries about how things were Denver came to the point.

"Dad," ventured Denver, "that letter I wrote is bothering me. It was written at a time when I was angry with God for letting mom die. I'm sorry that I took it out on you. You've done what you were convinced was right and you've been a good dad. It was wrong of me to send that. Will you forgive me?'

"Why certainly, Denver," exclaimed Roy. "You have just encouraged me immensely. There was also a lot of truth in what you said so don't beat yourself up about it."

"Thanks, dad. I've been thinking about my situation. I've come to the conclusion that the direction I'm going won't give me what I hoped for. These two that I am with are not a good influence. Parties and girls seem to be their main aim, I'm sick of that. I've been straying from what Jesus has to offer as the real thing. I need some solid maturing. I've decided to come home if I may. Maybe we can work together on this and you can help me find my place in life."

"Really!" exclaimed Roy. "That is super. I would love to have you come home."

"OK, dad, I'll be there soon. I'm thinking that maybe I can get involved with a few youth who are going through difficult times. I would be able to relate to them and perhaps help them work through it. I've already spoken with the fellow I worked for when I was at home and he's happy to have me come back."

"Wow, Denver!" exclaimed Roy. "That sounds awesome!"

"I'd need your help and insight as to how to work with troubled youth. OK?"

"Love to do that!"

"See you soon, dad, and I love you."

"Love you too, son. I'll be eagerly waiting for you."

A new sense of purpose and hope welled up in Roy. Perhaps the reversals of the last while had not been a waste of time. Maybe Teresa would turn her life around too. Roy could hardly contain his deep sense of joy. This was no time to give up. There were opportunities to reach out to Gary who really needed help right now. In addition there was the crew at work, people at the church, rebuilding his relationship with Denver and helping with youth work in the community and so on. Could there be some of the same seekers, opponents or apathetic men in this town that he or Denver needed to reach? He could only imagine. This is the time to become enthusiastic!

As he put Denver's letter back into his desk drawer Roy spotted another letter. It was one that Becky had written to him and given to Denver with instructions to pass it on to Roy after the funeral. It was such a caring letter. His eyes fell on one of the last lines again.

"Roy, darling, if it should be that in the future God would send along someone who will take my place I will be happy for you." **Was Becky thinking of Celeste? Maybe, just maybe....**

Appendix 1:

Three Aspects of Salvation

	Past	**Present**	**Future**
1. Time	1 Peter 1:3	1 Peter 1:7-9	1 Peter 1:5
2. Sin	penalty Eph.1:7 1 Peter 2:24	power 2 Cor.10:4 2 Peter 1:3	presence Eph.5:25-27
3. Family	position Eph.2:4-5, 13	condition 1 Peter 4:16-17 Eph.2:10; 4:1,14-16	translation Eph.1:10; 2:6-7
4. Theology	justification Rom.5:1	sanctification Phil.2:12-13 Eph.5:18	glorification Phil.3:20-21
5. Mind & Emotions	peace with God Rom.5:1	peace of God Phil.4:7	God of peace Phil.4:9 1 Thess.5:23
6. Nature	gift Eph.2:8-9 Rom.3:23	discipline Heb.12:4-6	reward 2 Cor.5:10
7. Christ	in Christ Eph.1:13	Christ in you Eph.3:17 Col.1:27	with Christ Col.3:4 Eph.1:14
8. Agreement	done deal	tough deal	new deal

Appendix 2

Guidelines for Learning

APPROPRIATE ACTION (and example)	KNOWLEDGE FACTS + I know - I don't know	ATTITUDES VALUES + I desire it - I doesn't desire	CONDUCT RESPONSE + \have the ability - don't have ability
1. **Control** (infant)	-	-	-
2. **Command** (toddler)	-	-	+
3. **Counsel** (marriage)	-	+	-
4. **Convince** (vice)	+	-	-
5. **Comfort** (sing)	+	+	-
6. **Confront** (clean room)	+	-	+
7. **Coach** (skill)	-	+	+
8. **Consult** (technology)	+	+	+

(Examples of how the above can be applied)

1. **Control** - Take a baby as an example. An infant doesn't know anything about facts and attitudes, nor does the baby possess enough abilities so the parent has to take **control**. We do everything for them and don't fault the baby for that.

2. **Command** - As the child grows to be a toddler one of the first expectations we have him/her is obedience to some simple commands like don't touch this or don't go there because the ability to respond to such a **command** is developing.

3. **Counsel** - A number of years later, when that child is getting married, the expectation is that the marriage will

work. If things go wrong it may be that they are blind to the facts in their relationship and unable to respond correctly. They want things to go well but they are low on facts and ability. But because the desire and the potential is there they can be **counseled**.

4. **Convince** - Suppose a teenager in your family is getting into a really bad habit. He/she doesn't realize what he/she is getting into. The teenager could overcome it but doesn't think it matters. So what's missing? The right information. That person needs **convincing** about the facts of the case. Lashing out would not likely work. But until he/she is convinced there will not be a permanent solution.

5. **Comfort** - Let's take another scenario, namely a person who knows the theory of music and wants to sing but does not show the ability. Try as he/she might the singing just doesn't cut it. What that person needs is the **comfort** of being directed into something for which they are gifted. Then they may be successful.

6. **Confront** – What about a situation where the child knows a clean room is required and is able to do it, but doesn't want to. Attitude is wrong and the child needs to be **confronted** about it. This is where we need to find out what it is that would motivate the kid. Is it challenge, curiosity, consequences, recognition, need or an appeal to become a caring person? Maybe it's a combination.

7. **Coach** - Now suppose a soccer player has the desire and the ability to play a good game but simply lacks the right technique or strategy. It is not attitude or ability that is the problem. Somebody needs to come along and show

him how. That's why there are coaches. He needs some good **coaching**.

8. **Consult** - Suppose you come across a person who has all three attributes. He knows the facts needed, has the right attitude and the ability to do the job. Say, for example, computer technology. In a case like that we can get them to show us how.

How are we going to keep this all straight in our head? It's kind of difficult but if we take these three aspects and the various examples we've discussed and draw up a chart like the one shown at the top, it should be easier. In the chart a minus sign means that aspect is absent. A plus sign means they do have it.

These principles are tough to apply in the heat, emotion or urgency of the moment. We probably all wish we had applied them more effectively while raising children. It is important to realize that these are guidelines. Few situations fit cleanly into just one category but these are good general guidelines.

Appendix 3
Prayer

Why Should I Pray?
1. God identifies with genuine prayer and loves to hear it.
   Is. 56:7 *My house shall be called a house of prayer.*
   Rom. 8:26 – 27 *The Spirit intercedes for us when we pray*
   Rev. 5:8 *God considers the prayer of saints to be like incense.*
2. God commands genuine prayer.
   1 Chron. 16:11 *seek His face always*
   Lk. 18:1 *ought always to pray and not give up*
   Jas. 5:13 *Is anyone in trouble, he should pray*
3. God promises to answer genuine prayer.
   Ps. 91:15 *call upon me in the day of trouble and I will deliver you*
   Jas. 5:16 *the fervent prayer of a righteous man is powerful and effective.*

How Should I Pray?
1. With integrity

Is. 58:9 Ps. 66:18 *clean up your act first*	Mt. 18:19 *be united*
Jer. 29:13 *be wholehearted*	Mt. 6:7 *don't do it for show*
Prov. 21:13 *be kind to the poor and needy*	Jas. 4:3 *have pure motives*

Jn. 15:7 *have faith that he will answer*   Prov. 1:23 – 28 *be obedient*

2. With purpose
   a. thanksgiving   b. praise   c. confession
   d. petition   e. intercession   f. guidance

3. With a plan
   a. Crisis cries of desperation for help
   b. Memorized or written prayers
   c. Structured lists in various categories
   d. Spontaneous expression of passion or burden
   e. Contemplative communion

Not only does the Bible tell the condition we should be in when we pray, but Matthew 6:9 tells us *'This is how you should pray'* It says **how** not **what**. This means that it is giving us a pattern or model that we could follow as a structured way of going about it.

PRAISE	'honored be Your Name' – vs. 9 Begin prayer with praise and worship.
PUBLIC	'Your will be done on earth' vs. 10 Pray for the leaders of our community, country and the world. In those places pray for those who are engaged in the Lord's work.
PARENTAL	'give us today our daily bread' This includes all that we need to do in order to provide for our own family.
PERSONAL	'forgive us our trespasses' Confession, repentance and forgiveness are needed. This requires us to examine our relationships.

PASTORAL 'deliver us from evil' Both the corporate and the individual ministries of the church body are designed to strengthen faith and weaken the impact of evil. Therefore this section includes all that the local church is doing as ministry and all that the individual is committed to as a ministry.

PRAISE 'Yours is the power and the glory' reminds us to end on a note of praise.

Appendix 4
Worship

The following are 6 possible ingredients of worship with a representative verse as an example for each one.

1. Admiring His creation with the wonder of an explorer.
   Ps. 95:3 - 7 *For the LORD is the great God, the great King above all gods. In his hand are the depths of the earth, and the mountain peaks belong to him. The sea is his, for he made it, and his hands formed the dry land. Come, let us bow down in worship, let us kneel before the LORD our Maker; for he is our God and we are the people of his pasture, the flock under his care.*
2. Acknowledging His power with the trust of a child.
   1 Chron. 29:11 – 13 *Yours, O Lord , is the greatness and the power, and the glory, and the majesty and the splendor, for everything in heaven and earth is yours. Yours, O Lord, is the kingdom; you are exalted as head over all. Wealth and honor come from you; you are the ruler of all things. In your hands are strength and power to exalt and give strength to all. Now, our God, we give you thanks, and praise your glorious name.*
3. Attending to His voice with the ear of a keen listener.
   Mt. 17:5 *While Peter was still speaking, the shadow of a bright cloud passed over them. From the cloud a voice said, "This is my own dear Son, and I am pleased with him. Listen to what he says!"*
4. Adoring His character with the devotion of a bride.

1 Chron. 16:28 - 29 *worship the LORD in the splendor of his holiness.*

5. Advertising His grace with the passion of the redeemed. Psalm 107:1-2 *Give thanks to the LORD, for he is good; his love endures forever. Let the redeemed of the LORD say this — those he redeemed from the hand of the foe,*
6. Addressing His work with the dedication of a true servant. Rom. 12:1-2 *Therefore, I urge you, brothers, in view of God's mercy, to offer your bodies as living sacrifices, holy and pleasing to God — this is your spiritual act of worship. Do not conform any longer to the pattern of this world, but be transformed by the renewing of your mind. Then you will be able to test and approve what God's will is — his good, pleasing and perfect will.*

Appendix 5
Excerpt on Making Decisions

1. Some things, like removing your hand from a hot stove, are necessarily **instinctive** reactions. There is no time for deliberation. The decision is pretty well made without thinking."
2. "That's the one," declared Jeb. "That's how this decision was made."
"Cool it, Jeb," complained Sam. "Let him finish."
Ever been in the shopping mall where you bought things that weren't on your list? You just acted on an **impulse** with maybe just a little bit of thinking."
"That's not me, it's my wife. She's wrecking our finances with her spending. It makes me so mad," admitted Harry.
"Harry, I didn't know you ever got mad. This is a revelation," laughed Sam.
"We all have our hot buttons, guys. Can we keep going?
3. Sometimes it's hard to get enough facts to make an informed decision but you also aren't happy with doing something on impulse. That's when a person may go on a hunch or a sixth sense. We could call that **intuition**."
"That's mostly for the gals," joked Jim. "It's a woman thing."
"Not always, Jim," countered Roy.
4. "The fourth one refers to decisions that should not be made without **investigation**. These are cases in which it is feasible to get the information. In cases like that, check the facts first. There is no excuse for hasty conclusions

when getting the real goods are within reach. Today's issue is one of those."

"Gary is the one that was hasty," objected Jeb, "We were not considered in this decision. We've got to protest."

"Jeb," answered Roy. "I'm not saying these things to instigate a protest. I'm just answering your questions."

5. A fifth method adds the benefit of experience to the investigating of facts. Investigation plus experience give us **insight**. That's why employers often ask prospective workers what experience they have had. Decisions are then based on experience and investigation.

6. Last, there are some things where we can only collect a few facts or do limited investigations. These are visionary plans that project into the future. For these we have the capacity to pursue abstract, intellectual reasoning to **imagine** what the results of various options might be when the foregoing five are not enough.

Therefore I think these are the 6 options we end up with. I'll scratch those 6 words into the dirt and you can think about it. You can use different labels but I've made them all start with the same letter because it is then easier for me to remember them. I believe each one is valid for certain situations. The first and last ones apply least often. Numbers 4 & 5 most often."

1	2	3	4	5	6
instinct	impulse	intuition	investigation	insight	imagination

"As usual," remarked Sam, "it's all so cut and dried. Who stops to think about these options and then chooses the best one? Not only that, it isn't always clear which one is best. People are too complicated and situations get complex so that everything gets murky. Your plan sounds good but is too hard to use."

Faith Under Fire

"Granted, Sam," agreed Roy. "It is tough to do things that way even when it is clear which one fits. Emotions take over and we don't even stop to think. It requires establishing a pattern of life that includes stopping to think before we act or speak. It's tough to hit upon the right approach on the spot. We don't know all that Gary was facing in this situation. We'd better find out more before we object."

Throughout the discussion Roy noticed that Jeb was taking notes. This was a change. In the past Jeb seemed to reject just about anything he said so Roy took some encouragement from this apparent change in attitude.

Two days later the subject came up again. The group pressed him to explain how he would go about telling a boss, or anyone else, how he felt about a decision that was made. After repeated pressure from a few of them he agreed to tell them how he saw things. Strangely enough Jeb was one of the ones who chose to listen.

"At both ends of the spectrum we have the most easily recognized ways of reacting to someone's decision or action," began Roy. "We can **lash out** with opposition or support the guy with **praise** or agreement. Smack in the middle is another common response – we **say nothing**. This may or may not be the right response. All of the options I mention can be right in certain situations. Sometimes rather than going to the extreme left of the scale by **condemning** someone, the right thing is to face that person directly with the issue, even if it means a **confrontation**. Talking to others about it without first going directly to the person involved is not fair. A still lesser tension may come in the form of giving a **warning** about possible consequences.

On the other end of the scale we may not be able to truthfully commend someone but they may well deserve **encouragement**. We don't always get it right but perhaps if we tried and are learning, a word of encouragement is just what we needed. It is also possible that someone just needed a clearer **explanation** of what's involved in order to do it right. They just didn't have enough facts or know how to do it. Lashing out at them is not the answer. Explaining is.

The problem with all of this is the same one that Sam told us a few days ago. It is hard to stop and think in the heat of the moment and choose the right response. Not only that, it's not always clear which one is the right one. However, this range of options can at least help us sometimes. So here is the list or range of choices.

1	2	3	4	5	6	7
condemn,	confront,	warn,	say nothing,	explain,	encourage,	commend

If we are doing it right, most of our responses should come under **explain** and **encourage** or even under **say nothing**. The fewest number (if any) should be under **condemn**. Whenever possible it is good to **commend**. At times we need to be up front with a person in a **confrontational** or **warning** mode. Does this make sense? In Gary's case the best plan might be to explain how we feel and listen to his side."

Questions for those who want to dig deeper.

Feel free to add or substitute your own questions.

Chapter 1 Moving
1. Are circumstances that work out smoothly an indication that God's will is being done or is facing hurdles, troubles and opposition the indication that we are in the will of God?
2. Are Roy and Becky doing the right thing for the family? Why or why not?
3. If you were Denver's parent what would you want to do to ease his adjustment in school?
4. Does Teresa's ease of adjustment carry any negative potential? If so, what might they be?

Chapter 2 Taking a Stand
1. Are the four options to those two contrasting questions valid answers for this issue? Can you suggest a better approach?
2. Was Roy wise in going this deep this soon? Why?
3. Why do you think Jeb stayed to see the diagram when he was so negative about Jesus?
4. Why is accepting or not accepting the Bible as the word of God such a major, watershed decision?
5. Are the three criteria for qualifying as God's Word accurate? What improvements in presenting proof on this issue come to mind?
6. How should Roy have handled his excitement without shelving needs of the family?

Chapter 3 Becky Speaks Up

1. What advice would you have given Roy in order to help Denver with his feelings of inferiority or Teresa with her desire to be looked up to by her peers?
2. Is it ever wise to step in and fight the battle for or with your son or daughter?
3. What does Denver need to do for himself?
4. What advice would you give Roy about his relationship to Sam?
5. Would you heed Sam's advice about not getting back to him about these issues? Why?
6. How would you avoid letting this get to you, clutter your thinking or rob you of time with your family?

Chapter 4 I'm Talking to You

1. Comment on the validity of those 6 C's as reasons for mankind's accountability.
2. Was Roy wise in giving Jeb such a full answer to his charge? What changes would you suggest?
3. What case would you make for the spiritual status of those who have never heard of Jesus?
4. Why did Sam defend Roy and yet also oppose him?

Chapter 5 Evolution or Creation?

1. How would you have responded to Tom and Harry?
2. Are there significant 'proofs' that Roy left out of his case for special creation?
3. What is your response to the idea of theistic evolution?
4. Is the conclusion they came to a valid way of ending the discussion?
5. How would you deal with the millions and billions of years that geologists talk about while the biblical account seems to suggest only thousands of years in the history of the universe?

Chapter 6 Dinner with David
1. What should Roy and Becky do now to help Denver?
2. Should the cost to your family serve as a restraint on your witnessing? Why or why not?
3. How would you answer David's claim about the separation of 'Christian principles' from 'business dealings'?
4. What is the most testing challenge to faith in this chapter?

Chapter 7 Family Time
1. What advice would you have given Roy about creating family times and improving relationships that are not already included in this chapter?
2. Should he have skipped the church service they happened to drop in on, or was this a blessing from the Lord?
3. Where is the balance point between the admonition of 1 Cor. 15:58, to *"always give yourself fully to the work of the Lord"*, and the needs of the family?

Chapter 8 Is God For Real?
1. Have you had any experiences of God's providential intervention in your life that you are willing to share with the group?
2. Should we rely on such events as proof that God exists?
3. How do you explain crises where we prayed and God seems to have ignored us?

Chapter 9 What's All This About Salvation?
1. Did Roy try to explain too much to Harry and Tom this soon? Why or why not?
2. Do you detect any flaws or shortcomings in this threefold picture of salvation?
3. Is there anything about God's plan of salvation that is still puzzling to you or presents some obstacles you just don't understand? Share them with the group.

4. How would you have gone about explaining the plan of salvation to Harry and Tom?
5. How would you resolve the problem of sinning after becoming a believer?
6. What is the balance point between addressing a person's physical, emotional and psychological needs as contrasted with his/her need for salvation?

Chapter 10 Suspicions Mount
1. Should Roy get involved in this matter considering what Denver said about David Tyler's son? Why or why not?
2. What is the Christian's responsibility when issues like this come up?
3. What risks is Roy taking?

Chapter 11 Gary Opens Up
1. How would you have responded to Gary's request?
2. Roy's response to Gary made it sound like Roy had it all figured out and under control at home when that was not the case. Should he have admitted that to Gary? Why?
3. What are the big limitations in using the chart Roy gave to Gary? (See Appendix 2)
4. What advice would you give Roy about how to balance your witness in the community with your service in the church and your relationships at home?
5. How would you have handled Teresa's invitation to the party?

Chapter 12 Seven Musts of Marriage
1. Is there any critical criteria missing from Roy's list? If so, what is it?
2. Is his PERFECT outline biblical or even wise? Would you be daring enough to assess where your marriage stacks up against this standard? (just for yourself)

3. How would you have responded to Denver and Teresa that night?

Chapter 13 Decisions! Decisions!
1. Was Roy right in offering his views on the decision-making process since it dealt with a sensitive issue that invited attack? Why or why not? (See Appendix 5 for questions 1 and 2)
2. Is the range of options in his decision-making process valid? What's missing?
3. What help or advice would you offer Roy in his despair over Becky's death?
4. How would you respond to Denver and Teresa at this stage in their lives?

Chapter 14 Struggling With Prayer
1. What is your definition of prayer?
2. Are the six purposes suggested in Appendix 3 comprehensive? (See #2 in that Appendix under "How should I pray?") Anything missing?
3. What do you do when you know you should pray but don't feel like it?
4. Do you set aside a time, a place and use a list for prayer? Why or why not?
5. Would you at this point have advised Roy to back out of any "whistle-blowing" role? Why?

Chapter 15 The Trap
1. What do you think of the tactics used by Harry and Roy?
2. How come Roy was so vulnerable?
3. If you were Roy or Harry, what would you do next about this case?

Chapter 16 Facing Crucial Issues

1. What is your definition of worship? What is the challenge to our faith when we think of worship?
2. What are some ways in which Christians worship rightly or wrongly?
3. What would you have done to prepare yourself for the "empty nest"?

Chapter 17 More Critical Issues

1. Was Roy dumping hastily on Sam with unrestrained enthusiasm or was it good to make Sam think?
2. What should Roy do, now that he has disappointed Denver again?
3. Did Todd handle employee fraud correctly? Why or why not?
4. Was Todd justified in rejecting Christianity on the basis of David's actions? What would you say to Todd?
5. What is the example of David Tyler saying to us?

Chapter 18 Surprises

1. How would you have handled the apprehensions Roy had about Denver's move?
2. What advice would you have given Roy regarding Teresa's decisions?
3. It has been said that faith under fire will eventually be ignited. Why would you agree or disagree with that statement?
4. How would you end the story if you were writing the last chapter?